contents

introduction

A lot of people pull a face when they hear the word 'greens'. Is it because childhood memories of being forced to 'finish up your greens' flash into their minds? Or is it because vegetables in general – and greens in particular – have a terribly dull image in this country?

Perhaps I should say *did* have such as dull image – for after *Grow Your Greens, Eat Your Greens* the image of vegetables will never be quite the same again. The series includes such a diverse range of committed, knowledgeable vegetable growers, each passionate about a particular vegetable, that you would need a heart (or stomach) of stone not to be infected by their enthusiasm.

Which brings me to the cooking. However zealous you feel about growing vegetables, it is easy to get into a rut over cooking them. In the *Grow Your Greens, Eat Your Greens* programmes, presenter Sophie Grigson pools her own extensive knowledge with that of equally expert cooks; the result is the treasure trove of inspiring ideas to be found in the book accompanying these series – *Eat Your Greens*, published by Network Books. Some of the recipes are unbelievably simple – why had I never thought of barbecuing sweet corn, or roasting asparagus, or making a soup from broad bean tops? Others are more adventurous; all are imaginative. As the vegetables come in season I know I shall be diving into the book again and again to revitalise my own cooking. The recipes and most of the cooking hints in this *Grow Your Greens* booklet are taken from Sophie's book. My thanks to her and to the publishers for allowing us to use them.

Each of the *Grow Your Greens, Eat Your Greens* programmes focuses on one group of vegetables – roots, squashes, onions and so on – and selects three representatives from each group. Those chosen range from familiar, everyday vegetables like carrots or leeks to more exotic plants such as aubergine and cardoon. Inevitably, many worthwhile vegetables have been omitted, and in this booklet there is only space to cover those featured in the programmes. See 'Further Reading' in the Resources section for information on growing other vegetables.

We hope that both the complete novice and the accomplished vegetable grower will find interest and inspiration in these programmes. The same is true of this booklet. For each of the vegetables covered we give the essential facts on how to grow a good crop, spiced with nuggets of wisdom from the experts visited. They have been so generous in revealing the secrets of their success that I suspect there will be quite a few eye-openers even for old hands. For the complete newcomer, some principles of good gardening and basic gardening terms and techniques are summarised.

Besides dealing with familiar vegetables, *Grow Your Greens, Eat Your Greens* has introduced a number of virtually new vegetables to the gardening public. Several of the oriental greens and salad vegetables, and the stunning red-fleshed Chinese radish, are making their television debut. They are all novelties worth trying. The Resources section gives sources of seeds and plants, and of the new materials and gardening aids – such as fleecy and net films and module trays – which are such a boon to vegetable growers.

As it turned out, the emphasis in the programmes and the booklet is on organic rather than chemical methods of gardening. Most of the gardeners filmed prefer to garden organically, and that is a fairly accurate reflection of vegetable growers in general – surveys have shown that today the majority prefer to grow vegetables without using chemicals.

The last word must be on taste. If you want the best possible flavour in vegetables, you must grow your own. Shop-bought vegetables never taste the same as home-grown. This is partly because of the varieties and methods used by commercial growers, and partly because of the simple fact that most vegetables start to lose their flavour the moment they are picked. The golden rule is the shorter the distance between garden and kitchen the better. In *Grow Your Greens, Eat Your Greens*, the emphasis is firmly on growing and cooking for flavour.

My thanks go to all the contributors to the programmes, from whom I have learned so much.

root vegetables

The root crops constitute some of our most nourishing and well-flavoured vegetables. Although many are delicious harvested young – carrots, beetroot, early potatoes and turnips, for example – the mature roots will keep for months and so are widely grown for winter supplies. Frost-hardy roots such as parsnips can be left in the ground, but most roots need to be lifted and stored under cover. As a general rule, root vegetables require good soil and a fairly long growing season to allow the roots to develop. Here we look at two of the most popular roots, potatoes and carrots, and the less well-known Jerusalem artichoke.

carrots

Carrots do well in all parts of the British Isles. They like an open situation and fertile, well-drained, loose soil which allows the roots to penetrate. Avoid very stony and very heavy soils. In many areas the main obstacle to growing carrots successfully is carrot fly.

Carrot varieties are divided roughly into two main types: 'earlies' are smaller, fast-growing and used for the first fresh crops or for forcing under cover; 'maincrop' types grow larger, mature more slowly, and are recommended for storage, though they can also be used fresh.

Cultivation
If possible prepare the soil the previous autumn, digging in plenty of well-rotted organic matter. Seaweed is excellent if you have a source. Carrots are difficult to weed, so if your soil is prone to weeds rake it to a fine tilth a couple of weeks before sowing, allow the first flush of weeds to germinate and hoe them off before sowing the carrots. Never sow in cold or wet conditions: wait until the soil has warmed up, then sow very thinly about 1 cm ($\frac{1}{2}$ in) deep in rows about 15 cm (6 in) apart.

Main sowings
For an early summer crop:
● Sow in unheated greenhouses, cold frames or cloches, or outdoors under fleecy films in February (in warm areas) or March.
● Use early types such as the round 'Paris Market' varieties, or the long 'Amsterdam' and 'Nantes' varieties

For the main summer crop:
● Sow outdoors in March and April.
● Use early types and maincrop 'Chantenay'

varieties.
For autumn use and winter storage:
● Sow outdoors in May and June.
● Use maincrop types such as 'Chantenay', 'Berlicum' and 'Autumn King'.

Spacing and thinning
Unless they have been sown exceptionally sparsely, carrots need to be thinned as they grow to allow them to develop to their optimum size. Paradoxically, early carrots, because they grow so fast, need to be thinned further apart than maincrop carrots. Thin earlies to about 10 cm (4 in) apart and, for a reasonable size, maincrop carrots to 4–5 cm ($1\frac{1}{2}$–2 in) apart. Thinnings may be large enough to eat. See also 'Facts about carrot fly' below.

Weeding and watering
Carrots are slow-growing and, particularly in the early stages, must be weeded between the rows or they will be smothered. They will only require watering in dry periods, when generous watering every two weeks or so should be sufficient.

Facts about carrot fly
● The carrot fly lays eggs at soil level. Small grubs hatch out and tunnel into the roots. In young plants, the leaves turn bronze and the roots fail to develop; older roots are disfigured and eventually destroyed by the grubs.
● There are several hatches of carrot fly a year.
● They are low fliers so can be kept out by barriers.
● They are attracted by the smell of crushed carrot foliage.

In areas where carrot fly is a serious problem:

● Avoid the worst attacks by sowing in March and June, when there are fewer adult carrot flies about.

● Since the smell of thinning attracts carrot flies, sow thinly so only minimum thinning is necessary. Thin in the evening, nipping off seedlings at ground level rather than uprooting them. Bury the seedlings in the compost heap.

● Grow carrots under fine nets or fleecy films, or surround the carrot bed with a barrier of clear polythene or fine net about 60 cm (2 ft) high.

● Lift maincrop carrots by October to prevent an overwintering generation developing.

● Never leave carrot debris on the ground: it will encourage the carrot fly to breed.

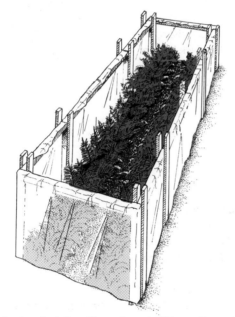

A barrier of polythene film or fine net will keep out carrot fly, the worst carrot pest.

Harvesting and storage

Pull young and maincrop carrots as soon as they are large enough. For winter use, carrots are normally lifted in October or November and stored in layers of sand in boxes in a frost-free shed. Only store healthy, undamaged roots. In mild areas with well-drained soil carrots can be left in the soil, where they will retain their flavour better than lifted carrots. After the tops have died down pull some soil around the roots and cover them with a 15 cm (6 in) layer of bracken, straw or litter. Take precautions against slugs.

> **Keys to success**
> ● Grow carrots in fertile, light, well-drained, stone-free soil.
> ● Sow thinly once the soil has warmed up.
> ● Keep carrot fly under control.
> ● If you have problems sowing carrots *in situ*, possibly because of difficult soil, try sowing in modules and transplanting when they have several small leaves.

Advice from our expert – *on sowing carrots thinly*

James Jamieson, enthusiastic carrot grower at Hyskeir Lighthouse, finds it is much easier to sow carrots thinly if the seed is mixed with a little sand. He sometimes sows radishes at the same time because the radishes germinate much faster than the carrots, so marking the rows and making it easier to weed in the early stages. The radishes are pulled for use when ready.

Use
Preparation for cooking
Mature carrots will require peeling, but young carrots need only be scrubbed clean.

Basic cooking methods
Cook young carrots in a minimum of water with a pinch of sugar, a little butter or a dash of lemon to enhance their flavour. Mature carrots can be sliced then boiled, steamed or added to stews. Carrots can also be eaten raw, either sliced or grated.

potatoes

Potatoes are often the first crop to be planted in new gardens, as they help to break up the soil, and soil pests such as wireworm invade them and are removed as the potatoes are harvested. They are greedy plants and, for high yields, must be grown in fertile, moisture-retentive soil. In small gardens it is advisable to concentrate on early potatoes as they take up less space and have such a superb flavour when home-grown. They are generally free from diseases such as blight which affect maincrop potatoes.

Potatoes are classified according to how fast they develop, starting with 'earlies' and progressing to 'second earlies' and 'maincrop'; the latter can be lifted for storage. There are many varieties, each with its own characteristics and preferred soil type. Experiment until you find which are best for your needs and gardening conditions.

Cultivation
Soil preparation
Potatoes must be rotated over at least a three-

year cycle. If possible prepare the soil in the autumn, digging in as much organic matter, such as farmyard manure, compost and old straw, as you can. Fork the soil over in spring before planting. A general fertiliser can be worked into the soil at this stage.

Chitting

Give potatoes a three- to four-week head start by sprouting them indoors or 'chitting' them before planting out. In February (or late January in mild areas), buy healthy seed potatoes that are certified as disease free and stand them in seed trays or shallow boxes with the end with most buds uppermost. Put the trays in a coolish room indoors in a light situation but away from direct sunlight. Charlie Maisey, four times UK champion potato grower, lines the box with a thick layer of newspaper, and once the potatoes start sprouting sprays them lightly every 10 days with the liquid seaweed extract Maxicrop. This helps them to develop very sturdy shoots and a mass of spidery roots. Plant the potatoes when the shoots are about 2.5 cm (1 in) long.

Planting

Start planting early varieties in late March or early April, provided the soil is reasonably warm and heavy frost is unlikely. Continue planting the later varieties throughout April and May. Plant with the sprouted eyes upwards, about 10 cm (4 in) deep, either in a drill or by making a hole for each potato. Different varieties require different spacing, but as a general guide plant earlies 30 cm (12 in) apart in rows up to 45 cm (18 in) apart, and maincrop potatoes 38 cm (15 in) apart in rows 75 cm (2½ ft) apart.

Early varieties can be protected with cloches or fleece films. The leaves may be damaged by late frosts: if night frost is forecast draw soil up around the base of exposed plants and cover them temporarily with newspaper or a light layer of straw.

Earthing up

As potato plants grow, tubers that are near the surface tend to get pushed up and 'greened' on exposure to light, so making them poisonous. To prevent this, earth up the plants when they are about 23 cm (9 in) high by drawing soil up around the stems to a height of 13 cm (5 in).

Removing flowers

Champions like Charlie Maisey nip off any potato flowers at the bud stage so that all energy goes into the formation of the tubers. The flowers are very pretty and can be used in flower arrangements.

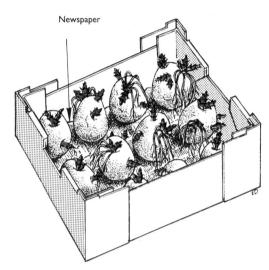

Newspaper

Spraying potatoes with liquid seaweed while they are chitting helps them to develop sturdy shoots and a mass of spider roots.

Watering and feeding

In dry conditions heavy watering helps to increase yields. Early potatoes can be watered every 10 days or so during the growing period. With maincrop potatoes, watering can normally wait until the flowers are forming: one very heavy watering at this stage can be most beneficial.

Yields can be increased by applying a nitrogenous fertiliser, or, for organic gardeners, a seaweed-based fertiliser, during growth.

Pests and diseases

Slugs can be a serious problem in some areas. The commonest disease is potato blight, which is worst in damp parts of the country. The leaves develop brown patches in mid to late summer, and the plants start to die. In damp areas grow resistant varieties such as 'Cara'. To prevent attacks potatoes can be sprayed with a copper fungicide in early July. Where plants are infected, cut off the foliage just above ground level in late August or early September to prevent the disease spreading into the tubers.

Harvesting and storage

Early potatoes should be ready to lift in June, 10–12 weeks after planting; they start to lose their exceptional flavour in July. Maincrop potatoes can be lifted for use fresh during summer and early autumn. Provided the plants are healthy, potatoes grown for storage can be left in the soil until September. Two weeks before lifting, cut back the foliage to allow the potato skins to harden. Dig the potatoes up on a dry day, leave them on the ground to dry for a couple of hours, then store in hessian or paper sacks in the dark, in a cool, frost-free place, giving them extra covering if severe frost threatens. They should keep until late spring. Never store damaged or bruised tubers.

Recommended varieties
For early crops and containers: 'Foremost', 'Pentland Javelin'. For flavour: 'Kestral', 'Vanessa'. For salads: 'Pink Fir'.

Advice from our expert – *on growing new potatoes in a rubbish bag*
With patio gardeners in mind, last year's champion potato grower Charlie Maisey grew a great crop of new potatoes in a black rubbish bag. He used the compact early variety 'Foremost'. Here is his method.

Prepare a rich, friable mixture of well-rotted manure, leaf mould and/or garden compost, all mixed thoroughly with potting compost or peaty soil from an old growing bag and a little general fertiliser. Puncture some drainage holes in the bottom of the bag and roll the sides down fairly flat. Put in several inches of the mixture and plant a tuber 10cm (4 in) deep. As the plant grows add more and more compost to support it, gradually raising the sides of the bag. Keep it well watered and spray weekly with Maxicrop seaweed fertiliser. The roots grow so densely that the bag may have to be cut open to pull out the potatoes 8-10 weeks later.

Use
Preparation for cooking
Just scrub or brush new potatoes to clean them. Mature potatoes retain their flavour best if cooked whole, slipping the skins off afterwards. If roasting, deep-frying or sautéeing, peel them first; if you are not going to cook them immediately, plunge them into cold water to prevent them discolouring.

Basic cooking methods
Steam or boil young potatoes. Mature potatoes can be cooked in numerous ways: boiled, baked in their skins, micro-waved, sautéed, roasted, deep-fried, and incorporated into stews, casseroles and soups.

Jerusalem artichokes

Jerusalem artichokes are grown for their knobbly tubers, which are roughly the size of potatoes. The plants are closely related to sunflowers and can grow over 2.4 m (8 ft) tall, so are often used to screen unsightly objects or to provide a windbreak. They can tolerate a wide range of soils and situations, and are very effective in breaking up heavy soil. They are perennial, and tubers left in the ground can spread. These are exceptionally prolific plants which are rarely troubled by serious pests or diseases. The tubers have an excellent, sweetish flavour.

Cultivation
Little soil preparation is needed, though poor ground will benefit if you dig in well-rotted manure before planting. Theoretically, Jerusalem artichokes should be grown in a fresh site every three or four years, but in practice they often perpetuate themselves on the same spot with little evidence of decline.

Plant the tubers any time from February to April or even early May – you can either buy them or save a few from the previous crop. Tubers the size of a small egg are generally recommended. Very large tubers can be cut into several pieces, providing each has a bud. Plant them about 15 cm (6 in) deep and roughly 30 cm (12 in) apart. They can be planted in groups or in a single row. If you want them to act as a windbreak it is advisable to plant them two or three rows deep, placing them on the north side of other vegetables so that they do not shade them from the sun.

Jerusalem artichokes require little attention after planting. In windswept sites earth up the stems to a height of about 30 cm (12 in) or so as they grow to make the plants more stable. It may be necessary to support them with canes and wire in mid-season. In late summer cut back the flowerheads so the stalks are no more than about 1.5 m (5 ft) high, concentrating reserves into the tubers. In the autumn cut the stems right back to within a few centimetres of the ground. (If you happen to have goats, feed the stems and leaves to them – they love them!) In very dry conditions Jerusalem artichokes will benefit from watering.

Harvesting and storage
The tubers can be lifted for use any time from late autumn onwards. They are very hardy so can normally be left in the soil until required; this helps to retain their flavour. Where severe weather is expected cover the stumps with a layer of litter

(the old stems can be used) to give some frost protection and make them easier to lift if the ground is frozen. For convenience they can be lifted and stored in a small clamp, but some flavour will be lost. Any tubers left in the ground at the end of the season will resprout and develop into plants, so remove them all if the crop is no longer required in that position. Smooth, medium-sized tubers can be saved for replanting.

Tall-growing Jerusalem artichokes make an excellent screen or windbreak.

Recommended varieties
Named varieties of Jerusalem artichokes are rare. 'Fuseau' has relatively long and smooth tubers; 'Sunray' is normally dwarfer than standard types.

Advice from our expert – *on keeping Jerusalem artichokes in check*
Performance poet Martin Newell delights in planting Jerusalem artichokes in the most uncompromising of corners in his garden in Wivenhoe. If he doesn't want them to spread, he sinks a bottomless bucket in the ground, fills it with soil and plants a couple of tubers in it. The roots will spread below the bucket to obtain nutrients, but will be prevented from spreading sideways.

Use
Jerusalem artichokes are notoriously 'windy', which may account for their being less popular than they deserve. Harold McGee, author of *The Curious Cook*, says they are less so after about a month's cold storage, either in the soil or in the fridge. Boiling sliced tubers in plenty of water for 15 minutes also reduces their 'windiness'.

Preparation for cooking
As the roots are normally very knobbly, it is best to scrub them and steam or boil them whole until tender or partly cooked. The skins can then be slipped off easily.

Basic cooking methods
Jerusalem artichokes have an excellent, sweetish flavour. Besides plain boiling for using whole or mashed, they can be baked, par-boiled then roasted, or sliced and deep-fried.

Stoved Jerusalem artichokes
Serves 4

1 kg (2¼ lb) Jerusalem artichokes
juice of ½ lemon
1 tbsp olive oil
25 g (1 oz) butter
2 tbsp chopped fresh parsley
1 large clove garlic, peeled and chopped
finely grated zest of ½ lemon
salt and freshly ground black pepper

Peel the artichokes and cut into halves, or quarters if they are large – the pieces should be about the size of a quail's egg or slightly larger. As you work, drop the artichokes into water acidulated with the lemon juice to prevent discoloration.
Drain and dry the artichokes. Place the oil and butter in a wide frying pan over a low to moderate heat and heat until foaming. Place the artichokes in the pan in a single layer. (If you have too many, cook them in batches or use a second pan.) Cover and cook for about 10 minutes, occasionally shaking the pan gently. Check after 5 minutes and turn them over carefully. After 10 minutes, remove the cover; the artichokes should be beginning to brown. Cook for a further 10 minutes until they are tender, turning occasionally so they colour evenly.
While the artichokes cook chop the parsley, garlic and lemon zest together very finely to make a gremolata. When the artichokes are done, season them with salt and pepper and sprinkle the gremolata over them.

---

the squash family

Courgettes, cucumbers and the large group of pumpkins and squashes are closely related vegetables, grown largely for their fruits. They all originate in warm climates so are tender summer vegetables in Britain. As a family they are naturally vigorous and trailing, so they require a fair amount of space unless they can be encouraged to climb upwards. Fortunately there are some bush forms more suited to small gardens. On the whole they are not highly flavoured or very nutritious vegetables, but they are fun and, given reasonable weather, easy to grow. The flowers and the young shoots, treated like greens, are also edible.

courgettes

Courgette is the French word for baby marrow (*zucchini* is the Italian), and that is what they are – left to grow larger they turn into the traditional marrow. Modern courgette varieties have been bred for harvesting young, and will give better results than would be obtained by simply growing a marrow and picking it young. Most of these courgettes are bush in form, so they are more suitable for small gardens than are old-fashioned trailing marrows. Provided they have reasonably fertile, moisture-retentive soil, they are easy to grow and very prolific – three or four plants are sufficient for most families. They should be grown in an open, sunny site, but avoid windswept situations and frost pockets.

There are many types of courgette. Those derived from long marrows are green, striped or yellow. There are also the pretty, fluted 'custard marrow' or 'patty pan' types, which look like spinning tops and come in white, yellow or pale green. Different again are the round forms, which are probably best when allowed to grow larger so they can be stuffed.

Cultivation
Work plenty of organic matter into the soil. Either spread a generous layer on the surface and dig it in, or make a hole for each plant about 30 cm (12 in) deep and 45 cm (18 in) wide. Work plenty of well-rotted straw, manure or compost into the bottom before replacing the soil.

Sowing
Courgettes cannot be sown or planted in the open until the risk of frost is past – which means not until mid-May in many parts of the country – so it pays to start them off indoors about a month beforehand. Sow seeds individually in small pots or modules in potting compost. Sow the seed point down, about 2.5 cm (1 in) deep. They can be started in a propagator or on a windowsill in a warm room, but they must have good, even light or they become elongated and 'drawn'. Sturdy young plants are the key to success. The ideal size for planting is when the seedling has two fairly large 'seed leaves' and a third true leaf starting to develop.

Harden off the seedlings carefully before planting them outside, spacing them at least 90 cm (3 ft) apart each way. For extra protection in the early stages, cover them with cloches or fleecy films. Alternatively, stand the plants in their pots under cloches at first to allow them to harden off further, then plant them out when they have four true leaves. If frost is forecast at night, cover any plants which are in the open.

Seed can also be sown *in situ* towards the end of May. Sow several seeds per site, thinning to one per site after germination. Cover the seeds with jam jars until the seedlings appear.

Courgettes have male and female flowers, which are insect-pollinated. The male flowers generally appear first; nothing can be done but wait for the smaller female flowers which follow and develop into courgettes. In some new varieties the fruits develop without pollination.

Watering, mulching and feeding
If there is dry weather after planting it may be necessary to water gently. Our expert courgette growers from Bath suggest watering early or late in the day but not in full sunshine, as the drops of

water act as a magnifying glass and can burn the young plants. This also applies to plants growing on a windowsill or in the greenhouse.

Once established, courgettes need very little attention. To keep the weeds down and conserve the moisture in the soil it is well worth mulching the soil with a thick layer of straw or similar material. In dry areas or light soils the plants may need extra watering. Watch for the soil surface drying out, or the leaves developing an unnatural blotchy look: that's the time for a heavy watering.

If growth is slow, give a supplementary feed. Liquid seaweed is widely used, especially from the flowering stage onwards.

Wrong stage

Right stage

Planting out sturdy plants is the key to good courgettes. Plant those with two strong seed leaves and a third leaf just developing, as in the lower plant. Don't let them become lanky and drawn like the top plant.

Harvesting
The first outdoor courgettes are ready at the end of June, and picking can continue until the first frosts. With regular picking a plant can yield up to 20 courgettes; the first few are often misshapen.

On the whole, the smaller the courgette the tastier it is, but the exact moment for picking is a question of personal preference. Cut very young courgettes with the flower attached and in bud. The next stage for picking is 'petal drop' – that is, when the flower drops off when the petals are touched.

Courgettes can be harvested up to about 15 cm (5 in) long, using the larger ones for stuffing. Press the skin to make sure it is still firm: old courgettes feel slightly soft, and are fluffy and floury inside. Towards the end of the season a few courgettes can be left to develop into marrows.

Recommended varieties
Green types: all 'Green Bush', and the many hybrid varieties, e.g. 'Zebra Cross', 'Tiger Cross', 'Ambassador'. Yellow types: F₁ 'Gold Rush'. Custard marrow: 'Custard White', 'Sunburst' (yellow), F₁ 'Scallopini' (green). Round types: 'Rondo di Nice', 'Tender and True'.

Advice from our expert – *on harvesting courgettes*
Octogenarian Henry Whitemore has more than 70 years of market garden experience behind him. Here's his advice on how to keep courgettes producing over a long period: 'Check your plants every day and pick any that are ready. If you don't cut in time you stunt the plants. If there's only one on you know perfectly well he can't be trusted . . . He'll take the lot and grow too big in no time.'

Use
Preparation for cooking
There is no need to peel courgettes. They are usually cut into slices before cooking. To bring out their flavour, sprinkle the slices with salt and leave them for 30–60 minutes. Drain and wipe dry or rinse rapidly under the tap.

Basic cooking methods
Sliced courgettes are best steamed gently until just *al dente*. They can also be fried, grilled, baked or cooked in a casserole. Adventurous cooks make them into a mousse – the dark green varieties will give the best colour. Very small courgettes can be boiled for no more than a couple of minutes, or steamed whole. Courgettes can also be scooped out and stuffed with meat or a vegetarian stuffing. Cooked courgettes are good in salad: toss them with a vinaigrette dressing while still hot, then leave them to cool.

outdoor cucumbers

The traditional long, smooth cucumber is a demanding plant that has to be carefully grown in a greenhouse with minimum night temperatures of 20°C (68°F), coupled with high humidity. Until relatively recently people without greenhouses had to make do with the more rugged, short, prickly-skinned 'ridge' cucumbers, so called because they were originally grown on ridges to ensure good drainage. However, plant breeders (notably in Japan) have developed an excellent range of hybrid outdoor cucumbers which reach a respectable length and are nearly as smooth as indoor cucumbers. Even more important for gardeners, they are extremely tolerant of cold temperatures and resistant to disease, key factors in growing cucumbers outdoors. Most people think they also have an excellent flavour.

Certain varieties of ridge cucumber are harvested young as gherkins. They are used mainly for pickling, though they can be eaten fresh. The juicy, round 'apple cucumber' is a curious form of ridge cucumber which can also be grown outdoors.

All types of outdoor cucumber should be grown in a fairly sheltered situation and protected from any frost. They are normally trailing plants, though a compact bush variety of ridge cucumber is now available. While cucumbers can be grown on the flat, trailing over the ground, they do better if trained or tied to frames, tripods of canes or some kind of support.

Cultivation

Prepare the ground as for courgettes, making a slight mound to ensure good drainage. Cucumber roots love to run freely through well-drained, humus-rich organic soil, so working plenty of well-rotted straw into the ground beforehand is particularly beneficial. Sow and plant as for courgettes: cucumbers transplant badly, so are best raised in pots or modules. Space plants at least 60 cm (2 ft) apart if grown on the flat, and 45 cm (18 in) apart if climbing. Take precautions against slugs in the early stages. Like courgettes, cucumbers are insect-pollinated. There is no need to remove male flowers, as is the case with some indoor varieties of cucumber.

Training

Cucumbers cling fairly well to supports, but may need to be helped with ties or wire rings in the early stages. They rarely climb more than about 1.5 m (5 ft) high. Where you want them to cover an arch (see *diagram*), nip out any side-shoots that appear in order to concentrate growth into the main stem; alternatively, you can train them in. When the main shoots reach the top of the supports either nip out the growing points or allow them to dangle down and continue growing.

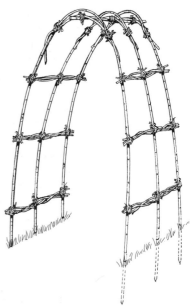

(Top) **An arch of cucumbers and climbing flowers.** *(Above)* **The arch itself made from whippy pieces of willow, woven together and tied with string and stripped willow bark. Bamboo or poplar could also be used.**

Watering and feeding

Once the flowers have formed and the fruits are starting to develop, cucumbers require regular watering if conditions are at all dry. Yields will be increased if they are fed with a tomato fertiliser or organic feed every 10 days or so.

Harvesting

Pick cucumbers in their prime while they are still glossy and before they soften or start to yellow. Pick regularly to encourage further cropping.

Recommended varieties
Hybrid outdoor cucumbers: 'Burpee Hybrid', 'Burpless Tasty Green', 'Tokyo Slicer'. Bush type: 'Bush Champion'. Gherkin type: 'Conda'.

Advice from the expert – *on producing vigorous plants*
Potter Janet Allan puts organic principles into practice in her lush, prolific and beautiful garden. On the willow arch leading into her vegetable plot cucumbers compete for space with sweet peas, climbing beans, pumpkins, canary creeper and nasturtiums. As the cucumbers grow she continually mounds up around the base of the stem with a rich mixture of soil and compost. This encourages extra roots to develop. To avoid washing away the soil she waters through several upturned plastic squash bottles with the bottoms removed which she spaces around the plant. The plants are fed in the same way with home-made comfrey liquid feed (see p. 43).

Use
Preparation for cooking
It is rarely necessary to peel cucumbers or to remove the seeds, unless they are being cut paper-thin for delicate salad dishes.

Basic cooking methods
Although cucumber is mainly used raw in salads, it can be cooked to make a delicate dish – for example, cut into wedges and simmered until tender, drained and then finished in a little butter. Cucumbers also make excellent pickles and soup.

pumpkins

It can be hard to know the difference between pumpkins and squashes, as they are members of the same family and it has to be said that the terms are used very loosely. Strictly speaking, squashes are summer vegetables, eaten at an immature stage (the common marrow is a summer squash), while pumpkins are autumn and winter vegetables, primarily harvested when mature and hard of skin. Depending on the variety, they can be stored for anything from one to seven months. Both come in an amazing variety of shapes, sizes and colours, and you really can't tell by the appearance which is a pumpkin and which a squash. Americans call all types of marrow 'summer squash' and pumpkins 'winter squash' – one of the sources of our confusion.

Most pumpkins are large, trailing plants, and most squashes grow on smaller bushes. However, there are exceptions in both cases, and several fall into an intermediate 'compact vine' category. Most pumpkins and squashes have beautiful leaves, and make very effective ground-cover plants. Trailing types can sometimes be trained up supports and arches, provided they are sturdy enough. Space can be found for them in small gardens by training them in a neat circle and pegging the stems down with wire or steel pins or sticks.

While the flavour of squashes tends to deteriorate with age, the flavour of pumpkins improves with maturity, generally becoming sweeter. The compact, dense, often drier-fleshed types of pumpkin tend to be far superior in flavour and cooking quality than the typical English pumpkin we have been brought up on.

Cultivation
For cultivation of squashes, see courgettes. For pumpkins, prepare the soil, raise the plants, water and feed in the same way as courgettes. Remember that pumpkins are generally larger and greedier, so dig in more organic matter and space the trailing types at least 1.2 m (4 ft) apart. Bush and compact vine types can be a little closer.

Pumpkins do their growing early in the season and colour up later. Small pumpkins generally start to ripen in August, and the larger ones in September. Move the fruits slightly while on the plant to encourage even development and ripening. Slip a slate, a board, or dry material like sawdust beneath the fruits to keep them dry.

Pumpkins can be grown in less space if the shoots are trained around in a circle. Pin them down with wire pegs.

Stem rooting

Keep pumpkins mulched with a generous layer of organic matter. Trailing stems in contact with the soil or an organic mulch will put out extra roots at the leaf joints, and these will supplement the plant's supply of water and nutrients. Encourage rooting by pinning the stems down. Towards the end of the season, nip out the growing points of the stems to concentrate all the energy into the swelling fruits.

Harvesting, curing and storing

Yields vary with type, variety and season. Large-fruited pumpkins may only produce four or five fruits on a trailing plant, or two or three on a bush. Small-fruited types may well have a dozen or more fruits per plant.

Pumpkins should be left on the vine as long as possible but should never be exposed to frost, as frosted pumpkins will not store. (If frost is forecast, cover any exposed pumpkins with rugs for the night.) Signs that a pumpkin is nearing readiness for cutting include the skin darkening and hardening (so that it cannot be pierced with a thumbnail) and the stem becoming corky. When they are ready to be cut the larger types sound hollow when tapped.

Cut pumpkins with at least a 2.5 cm (1 in) stem and place them in a sunny spot, exposed to the wind, for about 10 days for the skin to harden and cure. The harder the skin, the better they store. Store them in a cool, dry place at a temperature of 7–16°C (45–60°F).

Recommended varieties

'Acorn' types, 'Buttercup' types, 'Crown Prince', 'Hubbard' types, 'Kiri', 'Jack Be Little', Japanese types, 'Onion Squash', 'Queensland Blue', 'Rolet'.

Advice from our expert – *on when to plant pumpkins*

Ralph Upton has been growing pumpkins for a quarter of a century, and warns that they shouldn't be planted out until the soil temperature has reached 16°C (60°F). How does he judge this? He puts his hand in the soil. If it feels pleasantly warm and comfortable to him, he reckons it will be comfortable for the plant, too.

Use

Basic cooking methods

The best way to cook pumpkins is to bake them. Small pumpkins can be baked whole in a moderate oven. Cut off the top to make a lid, scoop out the seeds and fibres, replace the lid, and stand them in a little water in a baking tray. Large pumpkins can be halved or cut into wedges, removing the seeds and fibres. Wrap small sections in greased foil. Place large halves rounded side upwards in a baking tray to allow the juices to run out and cover with foil. Cooked pumpkin can be mashed or made into soup, pickles, marmalade, scones, pies and other desserts. Firm types can be roasted in pieces around a joint. Pumpkin seeds can be dried, fried in oil and eaten salted.

Chinese scrambled egg with pumpkin
Serves 2

175–225 g (6–8 oz) piece of pumpkin
4 eggs
salt and freshly ground pepper
2 tbsp oil
1 clove garlic, peeled and chopped
1 cm (½ in) piece of fresh root ginger, peeled and finely chopped

Cut off the rind of the pumpkin and remove the seeds and fibres. You should end up with about 100 g (4 oz) of flesh. Slice very thinly, then cut the slices into narrow batons 2.5–4 cm (1–1½ in) long. Beat the eggs, adding salt and pepper to taste.
Heat the oil in a wok over a high heat until hazy. Add the garlic and ginger and stir-fry for a few seconds. Add the pumpkin and stir-fry until lightly browned and tender. Pour in the beaten egg and quickly stir and scramble until beginning to set. Scoop into a dish and serve.

---

pods and seeds

Some of our tastiest and most nutritious vegetables are pods or seeds. Protein-packed peas and beans melt into our mouths while sweet corn woos us with its natural sweetness. How they are grown depends on their origins. Sweet corn, French beans and runner beans come from the Americas, need warmth and are more demanding than peas, which thrive with ease in our cool climate.

French and runner beans

French and runner beans are grown mainly for the pods, which are eaten young and green. In addition French bean pods can be grown to maturity and shelled for the seeds inside, which are dried as haricot beans; the semi-ripe seeds are used as flageolet beans. Beans are tender plants and need a warm site sheltered from strong winds and rich, well-worked soil.

There are both bush and climbing forms of French and runner beans. The bush types are earlier, but the climbing types are generally more productive. French bean pods vary enormously in shape and size, from thin and rounded to flat and broad, and may be green, yellow, purple or red-flecked. Highly recommended for flavour are the fine green 'filet' types, the smooth-podded yellow 'waxpods' and the purple-podded varieties. Runner beans have long, flat pods with a distinct flavour of their own.

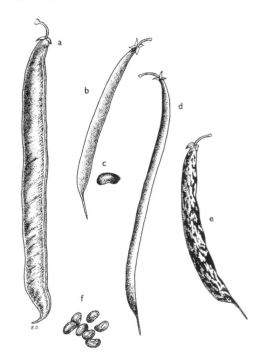

(a) Runner bean, (b) flat French bean, (c) immature flageolet, (d) filet French bean, (e) speckle podded French bean, (f) haricot beans.

Cultivation
Beans should be rotated over a three-year cycle. If possible prepare the soil the previous autumn by digging in plenty of manure or other organic matter. Most failures with French and runner beans stem from sowing too early in cold conditions. It is vital to wait until the soil has warmed up – ideally to about 12°C (53°F) – which could be as late as mid-May. Sow seeds about 4 cm (1½ in) deep in rows 23 cm (9 in) apart. Thin dwarf beans so the plants are eventually 23 cm (9 in) apart in the rows. They will benefit from being covered with cloches or fleecy film in the early stages. Beans can be given an early start by sowing indoors in seed trays or modules in April, planting them out after hardening off when they are about 7.5 cm (3 in) high.

To get a succession of beans, either make sowings at two-week intervals until the end of June or sow several different varieties at the same time.

When the plants are growing well push a few twigs between them to give some support and keep them from flopping on the ground. Mulch the soil with organic matter to conserve moisture and keep down weeds. In damp seasons take precautions against slugs.

Watering
French beans only require moderate amounts of water in the early stages. Once they start to flower, however, the yield and quality will be improved by watering heavily twice a week in dry weather.

Harvesting
Pick French and runner beans regularly to encourage further cropping. If you are growing them for the pods pick French beans as young as possible, while they can still be snapped in half. If they mature shell them and cook the pale flageolet bean seeds. For dried beans, leave the plants unpicked and pull them up in late summer when they have started to turn brown. Hang them

upside down in a dry shed or kitchen until the pods split open. Store the beans in jars.

Cultivation of climbing beans
Runner beans grow up to 3m (10 ft) tall so require very strong supports such as criss-crossed bean poles or tightly secured bamboo canes. Prepare the soil the previous autumn by digging a trench at least 25 cm (10 in) deep and twice as wide. Line it with well-rotted straw or manure before replacing the soil. Space the plants 15 cm (6 in) apart in rows 60 cm (2 ft) apart. Sometimes problems are encountered in getting beans to set. Grow them in a sheltered situation to encourage pollinating insects, and in dry seasons water regularly at the base of the plants after the first buds appear. Climbing French beans can be grown in the same way; dwarf runner beans are grown like dwarf French beans.

Recommended varieties
French beans
'Aramis', 'Delinel' (dwarf filet); 'Tendergreen' (dwarf green stringless); 'Purple Podded', 'Purple Queen', 'Royalty' (dwarf purple); 'Climbing Purple', 'Violet Podded' (tall purple); 'Kinghorn Wax', 'Mont d'Or', 'Roquencourt' (dwarf yellow waxpod); 'Marvel of Venice', 'Burro d'Ignegnoli' (climbing yellow waxpod); 'Barlotto Lingua di Fuoco' (climber, striped red pods, mainly for drying and flageolets); 'Red and White' (climber, obtainable only from the HDRA Seed Library).

Runner beans
Most climbing runner bean varieties are reliable and prolific. 'Gulliver', 'Pickwick' and 'Hammond's Dwarf' are excellent dwarf varieties.

Advice from our expert – *on growing beans the natural way*
Says the Reverend Wilson, 'You have to work with nature, rather than against it. Every gardener wants to extract the most they can from their garden and force the seasons a bit. But there's a law of diminishing returns which means the earlier you try and grow a crop the more work it is – and, equally,

the later you want to maintain a crop the more work it is. With beans my philosophy is to wait until the season is right and then put them in.'

Use
Preparation for cooking
Only use bean pods that are firm; floppy beans should be discarded. Top and tail them, and if necessary remove the 'strings' down the side. Fine beans can be cooked whole, but larger beans should be sliced.

Basic cooking methods
Beans must always be cooked rather than used raw, as they contain toxins which are broken down with cooking. Young beans can be boiled, steamed or stir-fried. Keep the lid on when boiling to preserve the colour. Older beans can be cooked more slowly in curries, stews or ratatouille. Cooled cooked beans are excellent in salads – mix them with the dressing while still warm.

French beans with cumin and almonds
Serves 4

2 tbsp olive or sunflower oil or 25g (1 oz) butter
15 g (½ oz) flaked almonds
1 small onion, chopped
450 g (1 lb) French beans, topped, tailed and cut into 2.5 cm (1 in) lengths
1 tsp ground cumin
salt and freshly ground pepper

Heat the oil and butter in a wide frying pan. Fry the almonds briskly until golden brown. Scoop out and drain on kitchen paper. Reduce the heat and fry the onions until tender, without browning. Add the beans, cumin and salt and pepper and fry for 3 minutes. Add 2 tbsp water, then cover and cook for 5 minutes or so until the beans are tender and most of the liquid has been absorbed. Return the almonds to the pan, stir for a few seconds to reheat, then serve.

---

peas Peas are ideally suited to our naturally moist, mild climate, and perform badly in hot and dry conditions. They require fertile, crumbly, well-drained but moisture-retentive soil. They should normally be grown in an open situation, though mid-summer crops will tolerate light shade. The true, sweet, pea flavour is only captured by home-grown peas –

surely the best reason for growing them.

There are many types of peas, of which the most popular are the shelling varieties. These range from 45 cm (18 in) high dwarf varieties to some growing over 1.5 m (5 ft) tall. Most seed is wrinkled, but some very hardy varieties used for early crops are round-seeded and less sweet. Unusual forms include the beautiful purple-podded types, and the tiny petit pois.

Mangetout or sugar peas have flat, edible pods, and a distinct flavour of their own. The recently introduced sugar snap is rounded, with the swollen peas more or less joined to the pod walls. They are exceptionally tasty and sweet.

Another recent development is semi-leafless types, in which the leaves have become modified into tendrils. This makes them almost self-supporting and, because they are extra well ventilated, very healthy.

For practical purposes, peas are divided into 'earlies', 'second earlies' and 'maincrop', reflecting the number of days they take to mature. The earliest varieties, which tend to be the most dwarf, take about 12 weeks, maincrops about 14 weeks. There is no reason why an early shouldn't be sown late!

Cultivation
Peas should be rotated over a three-year cycle. Where possible prepare the soil the previous autumn, digging in plenty of organic matter.

Sowing
Sow seed direct into the soil, but don't be in a hurry for the spring sowings; wait until the soil has warmed up. To get a succession of peas either sow at three-week intervals or sow a range of varieties at the same time.

Sow 2.5–5 cm (1–2 in) deep. Early sowings can be as close as 2.5 cm (1 in) apart to make allowances for losses but later sowings should be 5–7.5 cm (2–3 in) apart. Various sowing systems are used: narrow single drills, each about 90 cm (3 ft) apart; broad, flat-bottomed drills about 23 cm (9 in) wide, spacing the peas evenly along the drill; or 90–122 cm (3–4 ft) patches across a bed, with seeds evenly spaced 5 cm (2 in) apart. Seeds can be put in with a small dibber.

Main sowings
For early summer peas:
● Sow in March, or late February in warm areas.
● Choose a sheltered spot and protect with cloches or fleecy films.
● Use early varieties.
● Take precautions against mice (see 'Pests', below)

For maincrop summer peas:
● Sow from April to June.

● Use any varieties.

For an autumn crop (warm areas only):
● Sow in July.
● Use an early variety.

For a very early spring crop (warm areas only or in greenhouses):
● Sow October or November.
● Use hardy early varieties or mangetout types.
● Take precautions against mice (see 'Pests', below)

Supports
As soon as the tendrils appear all peas except semi-leafless types need to be supported. Either use pea sticks pushed into the ground among the peas, or erect sheep or nylon netting behind the row or around the pea patch.

Although not always easy to come by, pea sticks are the ideal way of supporting pea plants.

Mulching and watering
Once the peas are through, mulch them with well-rotted lawn mowings or organic matter to keep down weeds and conserve soil moisture. Once the flowers start forming, water regularly if the weather is dry.

Pests
The most damaging pests are mice and birds. Protect very late and very early sowings against mice by setting traps (cover them with tiles to prevent them hurting birds or pets). Dipping seeds in paraffin before sowing may also help.

Birds attack the emerging seedlings; cover them with pea guards until supports are in place. (Also see Gardening terms and techniques, p. 47.)

Harvesting

Pick shelling types as soon as the pods are plump, and pick regularly to encourage further cropping. Pick standard mangetout types when a tiny pea shape is visible inside the pod. Pick sugar snaps when plump and fresh green.

Recommended varieties

'Hurst Beagle' (early shelling pea for spring or autumn sowing); 'Hurst Greenshaft', 'Dark-Skinned Perfection' (maincrop shelling peas); 'Poppet' (semi-leafless maincrop); 'Sugar Rae', 'Sugar Snap' (mangetout maincrop).

Advice from our expert – *on watering to make peas weightier*

Schoolboy allotmenteer David Johnson watches for the pea flowers and the young pods to appear. At both these stages he starts giving the plants plenty of water to increase the yields and encourage the pods to plump out.

Use
Preparation for cooking

Whenever possible, pick and shell peas just before use to retain their flavour. The mangetout peas have edible pods, so just wash them and cook them whole if small or cut into sections if large.

Basic cooking methods

Fresh peas only need to be cooked for a few minutes; they are best boiled or steamed, but can also be incorporated into stews and composite dishes. Dried and ageing peas can be made into soup. Pea pods can be chopped up for soup or made into wine. Mangetout can be boiled or steamed, and are also excellent stir-fried.

sweet corn

Sweet corn needs at least a three-month growing season, plus warm, sunny weather in which to ripen. In northern and cool areas the best chance of success lies in using fast-growing, early-maturing varieties, or in growing it in a greenhouse or polytunnel. Sweet corn takes up a fair amount of space, but as long as the soil is reasonably fertile and there is plenty of moisture it can be intercropped with salad plants, courgettes, dwarf peas and even potatoes. Sweet corn does best on deep, fertile soil but tolerates a wide range of soil types provided there is good drainage. Avoid windy or exposed sites.

The best varieties for our climate are all F_1 hybrids; the late-maturing varieties are probably better quality than the earlies. Traditional varieties have recently been joined by the super-sweet types, which are not only exceptionally sweet but keep their sweetness longer after being picked. Their drawback is that they are slower to germinate and less vigorous. They must be grown in isolation from standard varieties, for they lose their unique character if cross-pollinated; it is therefore advisable to stick to one type or the other unless you have a very large garden. A few varieties of sweet corn are suitable for making popcorn. They are quite easy to grow.

Cultivation

Use ground where plenty of manure was worked in for the previous crop, as growth may be too lush on freshly manured ground. Sweet corn will not germinate outdoors until the soil temperature is above 10°C (50°F), which may not be until the end of May or early June. Sow two to three seeds per station, about 2.5 cm (1 in) deep, thinning to one if necessary after germination. Space plants 35 cm (14 in) apart each way, or about 25 cm (10 in) apart in rows 60 cm (2 ft) apart.

Sweet corn should be grown in a block formation to make wind pollination easier and so guarantee full cobs. Pollen is blown from the male tassels at the top of the plant on to the 'silks' attached to the seeds below. A gappy cob is one that has only been partially pollinated.

If sowing *in situ* it is advisable to cover the seeds after sowing with cloches, clear plastic film, perforated or fleecy film or fine nets (or even jam jars). Cut holes in clear plastic film to let the seedlings through; remove other types of film when the plants have about four leaves, and cloches when the plants are becoming restricted.

Raising plants indoors

It pays to start sweet corn indoors, sowing in gentle heat in a propagator or warm place. As the roots don't take kindly to transplanting they should always be sown in small pots or modules so there is minimum root disturbance on planting. The deeper the pot the better; a minimum depth of 5 cm (2 in) is recommended. (See our expert's advice on home-made pots, opposite.) Harden off well and plant out after all risk of frost is past.

When planting make a generous hole and plant the

pot about 5 cm (2 in) below ground level to provide some shelter from the wind. Work some sieved garden compost or good potting compost in around the pot, and as the plant grows level it off at ground level with more compost. This will encourage extra rooting from the base of the stem. Sweet corn can be covered with cloches when first planted and can also be planted through black plastic mulching film, which helps to retain moisture and keep down weeds.

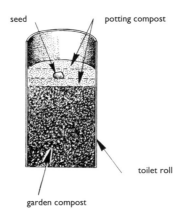

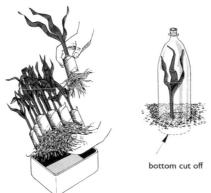

Recycling gives sweet corn a good start in life! Toilet roll tubes are ideal for raising plants; plastic bottles make miniature cloches.

Weeding, mulching and watering
Weed gently in the early stages, taking care not to damage the surface roots. Unless planted through black plastic film, mulch the plants with an organic mulch to keep down weeds and conserve moisture. Once sweet corn starts to flower (i.e. the tassels and silks become evident) a plentiful supply of water ensures a good crop. In dry areas and on light soils give the plants a generous watering once a week.

Harvesting
The average yield for sweet corn is one or two cobs per plant, though really well nurtured plants

may produce three. To tell when the cobs are reaching maturity, watch out for a certain 'fat' look and the tassels at the top of the cob turning deep brown. A further test is to strip back the husk a little way and pierce the top kernels with a thumbnail. If the juice is watery the cob is not yet ripe; if it is thick and doughy it is over-ripe; if it is milky it is ready.

Recommended varieties
Earlies: 'Butter Imp', 'Earliking', 'Sunrise'. Later crop: 'Reward', 'Sundance'. Supersweet: 'Xtra Early Sweet', 'Conquest', 'Sweet 77', 'Dynasty'.

Advice from our expert– *on how to make sweet corn pots from toilet roll tubes!*
Enthusiastic organic gardener Bob Flowerdew recycles all sorts of products in imaginative ways: for example, inner tubes of toilet rolls become plant pots (see drawing). He fills them two-thirds full with sieved garden compost, then a thin layer of bought-in sterile potting compost (to prevent weed seeds germinating). He firms this down and sows the seed on top, covering it with another layer of potting compost or peat or sand before firming again. He stacks the tubes side by side in a seed tray and waters them gently, taking care not to overwater them. They are planted out in the normal way, the tube rotting away in the soil in due course.

How to grow baby corn
- Select an early variety.
- Plant out 15 cm (6 in) apart each way.
- Harvest cobs when about 7.5 cm (3 in) long.

Use
Preparation for cooking
Use sweet corn as soon after picking as possible, as the natural sugars start to convert to starch within minutes. If it is being boiled or grilled simply strip off the outer sheath and silks and cut off any attached stem. The cobs may be left unstripped if you are barbecuing them. If you want to cook the kernels separately, stand the cobs upright and slice down the sides, close to the core.

Basic cooking methods
Whole cobs should be boiled for no more than 10 minutes in lightly salted water. Alternatively, grill or barbecue them. Kernels can be simmered in butter, or mixed into other dishes. Sweet corn freezes well.

the onion tribe

The vegetables in the onion tribe (which embraces leeks and garlic along with the many types of onion) have a distinct, much-loved flavour that plays a key role in our cooking. All flourish in our climate, provided suitable varieties are grown. Onions and garlic are available all year round, as they are dried and stored for winter use. The main season for fresh leeks is late summer to late spring; the hardy types are dug from the ground all winter. They can be frozen to fill the gap in early summer.

Mammoth onions

Large onions are among the specialities of the Lancashire seed firm Robinsons – fifth-generation Robinsons are now growing the 'Mammoth' onions originally selected by their great-great-grandfather. 'Mammoth Improved' has sweet, juicy, white flesh and the slightly smaller but stronger-flavoured 'Mammoth Red' has beautiful pink-tinged flesh. Unlike many large onions both store well. This is how they grow their onions: the methods used hold good for any other large onions.

Soil preparation
Onions require well-drained, fertile soil, though red onions seem to tolerate poorer soil than white. The key to successful onion-growing is to dig the ground over in autumn, working in plenty of farmyard manure or other organic manure. A slow-acting fertiliser like bonemeal can be dug in, but is not essential unless the soil is fairly poor. Leave the ground roughly dug and exposed to the frost during the winter, ideally ridging up the soil, then pray for hard weather. The Robinson family records show that the best crops followed severe winters!

In spring, fork or rotovate the soil before raking it flat. A general fertiliser can be worked in before planting, but avoid fertilisers that are high in nitrogen.

Cultivation
Large onions need a long growing season and are generally raised from seed (see 'Early onions from sets', opposite). The experts traditionally sow in late December (after Christmas) or in January, sowing in seed boxes in a greenhouse or propagator at a temperature of 10°C (50°F). Amateurs without these facilities are advised to delay sowing until February, when growing conditions have improved.

Onions like a firm soil, so if possible sow in a soil-based John Innes sowing compost. If unavailable, use a peat-based or alternative compost. Keep the temperature at about 10°C (50°F) while the plants are indoors; never let it rise above 13°C (55°F). Water gently to keep the compost moist.

The ideal time to prick out the seedlings is the 'loop' or 'crook neck' stage, when they are about 1 cm (½ in) clear of the soil, but still bent over like a shepherd's crook. They are still tiny so handle them very gently, spacing them 5 cm (2 in) apart in a seed tray of John Innes No. 2 or a potting compost. For prize specimens, select the strongest seedlings and prick them out individually into 7.5 cm (3 in) pots. If the crook neck stage is missed, delay pricking out until the seedlings have two true leaves and are altogether much stronger. Keep the seedlings well ventilated and take care not to overwater.

Onion seedlings at the 'crook neck' stage are pricked out from the small seed tray in which they were sown into a larger tray.

Before planting seedlings outside it is most important to harden them off well over a two- to three-week period. Plant outside from early April in warm areas, at the end of May in colder areas. Space the plants about 15 cm (6 in) apart each way. During the first few weeks after planting the onions develop and enlarge their leaves; once the days start to shorten towards the end of June, large onions divert their energy into developing the bulb.

Watering, weeding, feeding

Keep the ground weed-free between the onions. The large varieties need plenty of moisture for continuous growth, so water regularly in dry conditions to prevent the soil drying out. (Once onions get very dry the skins harden, and will then split if subjected to heavy rain or watering.) There should be no need to feed the crop once it is growing.

Early onions from sets

● Onion sets are very small onion bulbs; they therefore develop and mature faster than seed-raised onions.

● Only a few onion varieties are available from sets.

● For very early onions, plant 'Unwins First Early' from September to November the previous year. They will be ready in late June or July but will only store for a few months.

● Plant sets in shallow furrows and protect them from birds in the early stages.

Harvesting

Onions can be pulled for use fresh as soon as they are an appropriate size. For storage they must be dried thoroughly. In the warmest parts of the country wait until the leaves have died back before pulling up the plants. In good weather they can then be dried on upturned boxes outside. However, in cold and wet areas don't wait that long: pull up the plants while they are still green, generally in August or early September. Cut off the leaves 15 cm (6 in) above the bulb, chop off the roots, remove the rough outer debris and spread them out under cover in a dry, airy, preferably sunny place for several weeks – a greenhouse or porch is ideal. Make sure they don't get frosted.

Onions are ready to be stored when the outer skins are golden brown and crisp and the tops paper-dry. Plait them into ropes, store them in hessian sacks or

lay them no more than two layers deep in wooden boxes. If there is nowhere dry to store them, wrap them individually in newspaper. Store them in a cool, well-ventilated, frost-free place. Good storage varieties should last until well into April; some red varieties will keep as late as June.

Use

Preparation for cooking

Unless they are to be cooked whole, mature onions have to be peeled before slicing or chopping. The outer skins of very large onions can be peeled off and used first, leaving the inner skins for later. The paler inner skins of red onions become darker on exposure to light.

Basic cooking methods

Onions are mainly used to flavour a very wide range of dishes, from casseroles and curries to soup and relishes. They can also be cooked in various ways as dishes in their own right, for example simmered, baked, stuffed, candied or pickled.

The Robinson family soup

900 g (2 lb) onions (red onions will give a
    stronger flavour), finely chopped
50 g (2 oz) butter or margarine
2 tbsp finely sieved cornflour
1 litre (1¾ pt) meat or vegetable stock
    (preferably home-made)
3 bay leaves
freshly grated Parmesan cheese

Preheat the oven to 150°C (325°F, Gas 3). Fry the onions in the butter in a large, heavy-based saucepan until golden brown. Turn off the heat and mix in the cornflour with a wooden spoon, stirring continuously. Allow to cool a little before adding the stock gradually, stirring continuously. Bring the soup to the boil, making sure no onions are stuck to the bottom.
Pour the soup into a large ovenproof dish and add the bay leaves. Cover and put in the oven for up 2 hours. (The flavour seems to improve with a long cooking time.) Sprinkle with Parmesan cheese before serving. The soup freezes well.

---

garlic   Perhaps because of its association with warm foreign lands, there's an underlying assumption

that garlic is hard to grow in the British Isles. This is far from true: all it needs is well-drained soil and an early start.

The many strains of garlic have evolved in different areas in response to local conditions, and it does seem that after a few years a strain will adapt to the locality. If possible, start with garlic raised in the British Isles, or in an area with climate and soil conditions similar to your own. However, politely decline garlic offered from an unknown source: it may well be infected with a virus disease or nematodes (eelworms).

Plant individual garlic cloves that are split off from a garlic bulb. Choose British-grown garlic whenever possible.

Cultivation

Grow garlic in a warm, sunny, open site, rotating it within the onion group. It does best on light, well-drained soil, so if you have wet, heavy ground plant it on ridges at least 10 cm (4 in) high to improve drainage. Fork over the ground before planting. Sulphate of potash (or seaweed meal for organic growers) may be worked into the ground.

Planting

Garlic is grown by planting individual cloves separated from a bulb. Almost any clove will grow, but choose plump, shiny ones for the best results. The ideal size is about 1 cm ($\frac{1}{2}$ in) in diameter (or about 1 g in weight). Reject any that look unhealthy.

Garlic needs a long growing season; unless the soil

is very heavy or poorly drained, plant in the ground in October or November. Where this is impractical, plant from February to March, as soon as the soil is warm and workable.

Plant garlic cloves with the flat base downwards. Push them into the soil until they are at least 2.5 cm (1 in) below the surface. On light soils they can be planted up to 10 cm (4 in) deep (deeper planting gives higher yields). Various spacings are used: planting 18 cm (7 in) apart each way gives the highest overall yield.

Where the soil is heavy an alternative is to plant cloves individually in small pots or modules in October or November. Use an ordinary potting compost, or gritty, home-made compost. Stand the pots or modules in a cool, sheltered place outdoors during the winter. They will not be damaged by this – garlic is extremely hardy, and needs a cold period to stimulate growth. Plant out in spring, when the plants have developed a good root system and small green shoots. They may need protection from slugs during the winter.

Weeding, watering and feeding

Weed garlic by hand, especially in the early stages as it is easily swamped by weeds. Watering is only necessary in very dry weather if the plants show signs of wilting. There is no need to feed the plants at any stage.

Harvesting

Garlic is usually ready to lift from July onwards, by which time the plants are about 60 cm (2 ft) high and looking a bit 'weak at the knees'. Lift them when the outer leaves are starting to turn yellow but the inner leaves are still green. Delaying can adversely affect the quality and cause the bulbs to split up. The bulbs can be buried quite deep, so dig them out carefully with a fork. Shake or rub off the soil, always handling them very gently so they don't get bruised – any bruises turn to rot in store.

In dry, sunny weather leave them to dry outside for a couple of weeks, propped upright. In unsettled weather it is better to hang them in small bunches in an airy, sunny place such as a conservatory, greenhouse or garden shed, until the outer skins are paper-dry. They must not, however, be overdried or the cloves will lose their succulence. Once dried, gently rub off discoloured outer skins and any soil still adhering to the bulb, trim off the roots, and cut back any soiled or diseased leaves.

Garlic will keep from 6–12 months, depending on the variety and storage. Hang it by the leaves in loose bunches or plaits. (Moistening the leaves first makes them easier to plait). Where bulbs have disintegrated into single cloves, gather them together and hang them up in string bags. Garlic keeps best in airy, dry conditions at a temperature of 5–10°C (41–50°F). The cloves will start to sprout if exposed to moisture or condensation.

Advice from our expert – on finding the right garlic to plant
Herb and garlic specialist Rosemary Titterington advises that ordering garlic from a seed catalogue is best. If this is not possible, use garlic sold in supermarkets. Examine the packet label to see where it's from – English garlic should be your first choice, garlic from northern France is next best.

The strict importation regulations should guarantee its healthiness.

Use
Preparation for cooking
The most important thing to know about garlic is that the finer it is cut, the stronger the flavour. It is most pungent of all when squeezed, and least pungent when cooked whole. To peel garlic, knock one side with a kitchen knife or cleaver. The skin then breaks away easily.

Basic cooking methods
Garlic is used in countless ways to flavour dishes. It is, for example, the perfect starting point for a stir-fry of oriental greens (see p. 26). It can also be baked whole, puréed with onion, and pickled.

leeks

Leeks are popular not just because they are fairly easy to grow but also because the hardy varieties provide a welcome change from root vegetables and brassicas in winter. The famous giant leek competitions produce specimens of amazing length and girth, but what cooks want are medium-sized, manageable leeks, which are far better flavoured. For a very delicate flavour, grow the young, thin 'mini-leeks'. Most cooks also appreciate the tenderness of a long, white shaft in a leek, encouraged by deep planting or blanching. Fortunately, culinary leeks seem to be much healthier and easier to grow than show leeks. Varieties of the former range from those with a long white shaft and generally light green leaves (known as 'flags') to short, stocky types with darker green or nearly blue leaves and a shorter white shaft. As a rule the tall types are earlier maturing, and the shorter types – including the famous 'pot leeks' - are later maturing, hardier and grown for winter and early spring. Sowing two or three varieties in succession guarantees a steady supply from late summer onwards.

Cultivation
Leeks must have deep, rich, well-manured, loose soil. Dig it over the previous autumn, working in plenty of farmyard manure or compost. Very acid soils will need liming.

Leeks cannot be sown in situ outdoors until the soil has warmed up to about 7°C (44°F), generally in March. Sow an early variety first, continuing with later varieties in April and early May. Sow thinly 2.5 cm (1 in) deep in drills, thinning seedlings

out to 4 cm (1.5 in) apart. Transplant them into their permanent positions from June onwards, when they are about 20 cm (8 in) high, and, ideally, pencil-thick.

Alternatively, start leeks off indoors in late February or early January. Sow in a heated propagator in the same way as large bulb onions (see p. 18). Harden off carefully before planting out, protecting them from frost at night if necessary.

Planting
Leeks can be planted from May until early August. To encourage a long white shaft, they are either planted in deep holes or planted on the flat and later earthed up. The first method is simpler and most widely used.

Water the ground first if it is dry, then make a hole 15–20 cm (6–8 in) deep with a dibber and drop the leek in. Trim off the leaf tips, as they are apt to become diseased if they drag on the soil. Traditionally the roots were also trimmed back, as it was believed this helped the leeks 'get away'. Some research has indicated this may not be true: adventurous gardeners may like to experiment and see who is right.

To get average-sized leeks, space them 15 cm (6 in) apart in rows 30 cm (12 in) apart. Closer spacing will give smaller leeks. (See also 'Mini-leeks', below.)

Water gently into the holes, leaving the soil to fill

in around the root as it grows. Leeks require little further attention, though later in the season, soil can be pulled up around the stems as they grow, to blanch them further. They like plenty of moisture, so water to prevent them becoming dried out. If this happens, they run to seed and the stems harden unpleasantly.

Harvesting
Pull leeks as required as soon as they reach a usable size. The hardy varieties can be left in the ground all winter and dug out when needed.

(Left) Large leeks are grown well spaced out, often planted in deep holes. *(Right)* Small, tasty 'mini-leeks' are grown much closer, on the flat, and are harvested young.

Heeling in
Leeks are often in the ground for six months or more. If the ground they are occupying is needed for another crop in spring, lift them up and heel them into a shallow trench in an out-of-the-way spot. Place them on their sides and cover them lightly with soil. This also delays the process of running to seed.

Growing mini-leeks
Dobies Seeds trialled various leeks for growing as mini-leeks and found the long-shafted 'King Richard' was the most suitable. They can be grown very close, say in rows 7.5 cm (3 in) apart. Sow the seeds evenly no more than 0.5–1 cm ($^1/_4$–$^1/_2$ in) apart so there is no need to thin. They can be pulled about 13 weeks later, when they are 15–20 cm (6–8 in) tall. Both the solid centre and the leaves will be tender, and can be used raw in salad or lightly cooked in oil or butter.

Recommended varieties
Early (ready September to December): 'King Richard', 'Gennevilliers Splendid', 'Autumn Mammoth Pancho', 'Lyon Prizetaker' (previously 'Sutton's Prizetaker'). Late (ready December to April): 'Autumn Mammoth Goliath', 'Musselburgh', 'Cortina', 'Winter Crop'.

Note that cropping seasons are only approximations, depending on the variety, the area and the season. There are many other excellent varieties.

Advice from our expert – *on looking after leeks*
Davy Conroy lives for the Northumberland leek shows but also loves to grow leeks for cooking; convinced they appreciate attention, he watches over them carefully. His general advice is: 'Basically, keep them watered and give them a liquid feed of seaweed (Maxicrop) once a week during the summer.'

Use
Preparation for cooking
Cleaning leeks thoroughly is essential, as earth is apt to become lodged deep down between the leaves. Trim off the coarse top part of the leaves, slice the leek down the centre beyond the halfway point and wash it under the tap, splaying it out to flush soil out of all crevices. It can then be cut as the recipe requires.

Basic cooking methods
With their gentle but distinct flavour, leeks can be used much like onions to flavour a wide range of dishes. There is also tremendous scope for using them as a cooked vegetable: they can be boiled briefly, steamed, braised, stir-fried, creamed and sautéed as well as constituting the key ingredient in quiches, soups, casseroles and, of course, leek pudding. Cooked and cooled leeks make a most tasty salad.

> **Tip for flower arrangers**
> In late spring, allow a few leeks to run to seed – the flowerheads are stunning in the garden or as a fresh or dried cut flower. Cut them while they still have colour. For dried flowers, simply stand them in a dry container indoors.

greens

Those vegetables loosely known as 'greens' are the mainstay of our kitchen gardens. Almost without exception they require fertile soil if they are to flourish, but apart from that, they vary in the skills required from the gardener. *Grow Your Greens, Eat Your Greens* looked at cauliflower, a demanding but very familiar vegetable; the beautiful, easily grown but less well-known ruby chard; and an exciting new range of greens from China and Japan which are at their best in the winter months.

Swiss chard

Few vegetables are such good value as Swiss chard, which goes by a number of names including silver beet, seakale beet and leaf beet. Mature plants have very broad leaf stalks and midribs, both of which can be pure white, deep red or creamy in colour. The leaves are large, glossy and crinkled, again varying in colour from red to bronze, deep green and a light green verging on yellow. Both leaves and stems are edible, making it virtually two vegetables in one.

The chards are healthy and handsome, surviving most winters outdoors and being available for picking over a very long period – all of which makes them excellent vegetables to plant in flower beds, either singly or in groups.

The best-known Swiss chards are the green-leaved types. The striking red-leaved, red-stemmed 'Ruby' or 'Rhubarb' chard has less drought resistance than green chards and a tendency to bolt prematurely. However, next year the seed merchant S. E. Marshall (see p. 55) are introducing a spectacular new variety, 'Feurio', which appears to have excellent bolting resistance.

Cultivation
The main requirement is an open site and fertile, moisture-retentive soil into which plenty of well-rotted manure or compost has been worked.

Sowing
With two sowings it is possible to have an all-year-round supply of chard, though crops in the ground outdoors in winter normally need some sort of protection, such as cloches or films. March or April sowing will give supplies in summer and late into autumn. In a mild winter the plants will remain in a reasonable state and start growing again in spring before running to seed in early summer. Plants sown in June or July will start cropping in late autumn, and will continue to crop well into summer the following year. In late summer, plant a few young plants in an unheated greenhouse: they will start growing early in the year when greens are in short supply.

Chard can either be sown direct in the soil and thinned to its final spacing, or sown indoors in seed trays or modules and transplanted to its permanent position a month or so later. Space it 23–30 cm (9–12 in) apart; the wider the spacing, the larger the plants will grow. Watch out for slug damage in the early stages.

Nothing is wasted with Swiss chard. *(Top)* Small young leaves are used whole in salad. *(Above)* With mature leaves, the broad stems and leafy parts are cooked as two separate vegetables.

Watering feeding, mulching

Mulch chards with an organic mulch, and give them an occasional liquid feed during the summer. In dry conditions water ruby chard regularly to prevent bolting.

Harvesting

Start cutting individual leaves as soon as they are a usable size. New leaves develop rapidly. At the end of their season plants run to seed, but the immature flowerheads are quite tender and can also be eaten. The red chards look quite spectacular when seeding.

Recommended varieties

Green-leaved varieties: 'Fordhook Giant', 'Lucullus'. Red-leaved varieties: 'Ruby Chard', 'Feurio' (available 1994).

Advice from our expert – *on using up old seed*

Sculptor Richard Logan grows ruby chard because he loves both its flavour and its vibrant looks. He 'station sows' *in situ*, initially sowing seeds in groups 10–13 cm (4–5 in) apart. He has discovered that the seed remains viable for several years. Rather than throwing away old packets he just sows them a little closer, thinning to the correct spacing when they germinate.

Use
Preparation for cooking

Slice the stems diagonally into 1 cm (^{1}/$_2$ in) wide strips, pulling off any tough strings. Cut out the midribs with a sharp knife and prepare them similarly. Shred or slice large leaves, run them under a tap and shake off the water before cooking.

Basic cooking methods

The stems and leaves can be cooked separately or together; in the latter case start the stems 5–10 minutes before the leaves. They can be steamed, sweated in a little oil or butter, stir-fried, sautéed, or used in casseroles, tarts, pizzas and gratins. The stems and midribs can be served with dips such as asparagus, while the leaves can be used as a wrapping for fish or meat. All spinach recipes can be used for chard leaves. Very tender young leaves can be eaten raw in salads.

oriental greens

For anyone who loves leafy vegetables, the oriental greens are a treasure trove waiting to be explored. They come from China and Japan, and because the seed of many varieties was not available here until very recently British gardeners are only now beginning to grow them. Most of them are brassicas – members of the cabbage family. Chinese cabbage is the best known, but is probably one of the most difficult to grow.

These greens have several advantages over the old British favourites. For a start, they are far more vigorous and faster-growing than our traditional brassicas. Some can be harvested within two months of sowing – even sooner if they are cut young. Most of them naturally grow best in late summer and early autumn, and the hardy ones, such as the mustards, komatsuna and mizuna, happily survive most winters outdoors, giving pickings right through into spring. So, if sown from late June to August, they fit neatly into the average vegetable garden, following on after lifting the early potatoes, peas and salads. Being very productive, they are particularly good value in small gardens.

Many of the oriental greens grow into handsome plants. Some of the mustards have striking purple leaves; mizuna has glossy deep green, saw-edged leaves; rosette pak choi makes a stunning, star-like pattern; and the creamy centres of 'Ruffles' fluffy-top cabbage are very eye-catching in summer. Not only do they look attractive growing in the vegetable plot, they can be planted into flower beds or decorative potagers with great effect.

The most important thing about vegetables, of course, is their flavour, and within this group there is an amazing range. Chinese cabbage is relatively bland; the pak chois are slightly stronger flavoured; Chinese broccoli and other types grown for the flowering shoots are quite sweet; komatsuna, mizuna and mibuna have distinctive flavours, while the mustards can be hot and almost spicy.

Harvesting

One of the characteristics of the oriental greens is that most of them can be harvested at various stages, from seedling to flowering shoot.

Cut-and-come-again seedlings

If seed is sown fairly thickly the young seedlings can be cut when 5–10 cm (2–4 in) tall, just above the first small seed leaves. They usually regrow within a few days, giving a second, sometimes even a third cut over a few weeks. The young seedlings are very tasty and nutritious, especially if eaten raw in salads. They can be sown in very small spaces, and even in containers.

Semi-mature harvesting

The leafy oriental greens can be cut at any stage before they mature. The pak chois, for example, can be harvested as neat little plants 10–13 cm (4–5 in) high, rather than leaving them to develop into large plants. This is useful when a quick crop is required.

Almost any of the leafy greens, if cut about 4 cm (1½ in) above ground level at any stage, will throw out a succession of leaves over a long period. This can be very useful in winter, as plants that have been cut back have more resistance to frost than large leafy plants. Plants transplanted into unheated greenhouses or frames in the autumn can be cut back regularly and will continue producing fresh greens all through winter into spring.

Mature harvesting

Harvesting can also wait until the plant is fully grown. Even then, cut off the head 2.5 cm (1 in) or so above ground rather than pulling it up. The stump will sprout green leaves which can be used over several weeks.

Flowering shoots

Several oriental brassicas, such as choy sum, flowering rape 'Bouquet' and Chinese broccoli, are grown mainly for the young flowering shoots, rather like our purple sprouting broccoli. However, there comes a time when all oriental greens run to seed and produce flowering shoots. The mustard shoots tend to be peppery hot, but the others are surprisingly sweet and can be eaten raw in salads or cooked. Pick them before the flowers open and keep picking to encourage more shoots to develop. Once they start to get tough the plants should be pulled up.

Cultivation

The oriental greens need very fertile soil and plenty of moisture throughout growth. Dig as much organic matter into the soil as possible and, once the plants are growing well, keep the soil mulched, either with an organic or plastic mulch.

Sowing

Unfortunately many oriental greens run to seed rapidly if sown early in the year, either because temperatures are low or because of the daylength, or sometimes because of a combination of factors. Although there are exceptions and some bolt-resistant varieties, as a general rule delay sowing until mid-June (when the days will soon be getting shorter), and continue sowing in July and early August.

Cut-and-come-again seedling crops can be sown in spring as they will be cut before the plants run to seed. Sow in February in greenhouses or frames, continuing outdoors as soon as the soil is workable. Late sowings of seedling crops can be made outside in September, and in greenhouses or frames in early October. All these are especially useful sowings, as they come in when fresh greens are scarce.

Sowing cut-and-come-again seedlings

The best method is to sow in flat, shallow drills. Make a 10 cm (4 in) wide drill, about 2 cm (¾ in) deep, with the blade of an onion hoe or draw hoe.

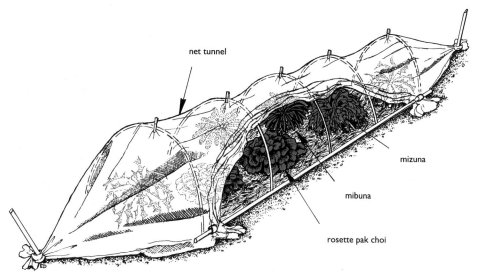

net tunnel

mizuna

mibuna

rosette pak choi

Oriental greens grow exceptionally well under fine nets, which both protect them from insect pests and provide shelter.

If the weather is dry water the bottom of the drill before sowing the seed as evenly as possible across the drill. Aim to space the seeds about 1 cm ($\frac{1}{2}$ in) apart. Gently cover with soil. The next drill can be as close to the first as you can make it.

Sowing single plants
Plants that will be grown to maturity can be sown in drills *in situ*. Thin in stages to the recommended spacing for the type and variety. The thinnings can often be eaten.

Alternatively, sow seeds indoors in seed trays and transplant outside. Sowing in modules or small pots is highly recommended for oriental greens and lessens the risk of bolting after they are planted.

Pests and diseases
The Chinese greens are susceptible to the same problems as European brassicas (see p. 27). In the young stages slugs can be a severe problem, and it pays to hunt for them at night. Chinese greens respond exceptionally well to being grown under fine nets, which both keep out many potential pests and give shelter from wind.

Recommended oriental greens
Chinese cabbage 'Kasumi'. Fluffy-top Chinese cabbage 'Ruffles' (earlier known as 'Eskimo'). Pak choi 'Shanghai', 'Joi Choi' and rosette pak choi. Komatsuna 'Tendergreen'; mizuna and mibuna. Mustards 'Green-in-the-Snow', 'Amsoi' and 'Red Giant'. Chinese broccoli 'Gai Laan'. Flowering greens 'Bouquet'. You could also try 'Oriental Saladini', a seed mixture of six oriental greens which was developed to give gardeners new to oriental greens the opportunity to get the feel of them. They can be sown as a cut-and-come-again seedling crop, or individual plants can be singled out and grown to maturity.

Use
Basic cooking methods
Oriental greens have such subtle flavours they are best steamed or stir-fried rather than boiled. A selection of oriental greens stir-fried together becomes a wonderful blend of flavours and textures.

They can also be made into soup or incorporated into other recipes. Young leaves are excellent in salads with conventional or oriental dressings.

Stir-frying
Stir-frying is an easily mastered art, and a wonderful way of cooking many vegetables. Not only is it quick, it also preserves their nutrients and flavour. It is easiest to stir-fry in a wok, but if you haven't got one make do with a large frying pan, a deep-sided sautéeing pan or a heavy saucepan. Oriental greens can be stir-fried on their own or mixed with any other vegetables in season.

● Cut leafy parts into pieces roughly 5–7.5 cm (2–3 in) long and stalks (and podded or root vegetables) into pieces about 2.5 cm (1 in) long.
● Heat the wok or pan until it starts to smoke.
● Put in 2–3 tbsp of oil. For leafy greens, use approximately 1 tbsp of oil per handful of greens. Use a mild-flavoured oil such as a blended vegetable oil rather than strong-flavoured oils like olive oil. (Sesame oil is the exception, as it blends well with oriental vegetables.)
● Swirl the oil in the base of the wok or pan and up the sides.
● Put in a sliced garlic clove, cook it gently until it sizzles, then add a little sliced fresh ginger, similarly heating it until it sizzles. Garlic and ginger are not essential, but add a unique quality to the greens.
● Add the prepared vegetables, putting the stalks, root vegetables and pods in first, followed by the leafy parts half a minute later. Toss them around for 30–60 seconds until they are well coated in oil and partially cooked.
● Add other seasonings according to taste, such as sea salt, ground pepper, herbs, chopped onions.
● If the mixture is dry add a little moisture. It can be water, white wine, stock, or soya sauce diluted in a little water.
● Cook until the vegetables are tender but crisp. This normally takes no more than a few minutes, depending on the vegetables and the quantities involved. If the vegetables are thick and bulky, cover the pan for this stage. It is unnecessary for small quantities.

cauliflower

Cauliflowers are members of the brassica family, which includes cabbages, brussels sprouts and kales. They are all large, leafy plants, requiring very fertile but firm soil. Cauliflowers don't require as rich a soil as other brassicas, but they must have adequate moisture throughout their growth; the commonest cause of failure is lack of water. Working plenty of organic matter into the soil beforehand and keeping the soil mulched with a layer of straw or compost at least 5 cm (2 in) thick is the best way to retain moisture in the soil and get a good crop. Very acid soils should be limed.

Cauliflowers take up a fair amount of space over 6–12 months, so are best suited to large gardens. Small gardens, however, can grow mini-cauliflowers.

Cauliflowers are grouped roughly according to when they mature, and can be harvested almost all year round provided suitable varieties are sown at the right time. When it comes to flavour, freshly picked caulis are a world apart from bought ones. Undoubtedly the best flavoured of all are the green- and purple-headed types.

Cultivation

Rotate cauliflowers in the brassica group, growing them in ground where plenty of organic manure was dug in for the previous crop. Don't fork over the soil before planting: just rake and clear it.

Sowing

Cauliflowers are normally sown in a seedbed outdoors. They can also be raised in modules or small pots, or sown *in situ* and thinned to the correct spacing. They should be transplanted no later than six weeks after sowing.

Planting

Make sure the soil is moist when planting and plant firmly, using the correct spacing for the group as given in the table above. The earliest plantings can be protected with cloches or fleecy films. From late spring onwards mulch the plants generously to retain soil moisture.

Mini-cauliflowers

These are grown very close so the heads are no more than 4–7.5 cm (1½–3 in) in diameter. Use an early summer variety and sow or plant so that the plants are only 15 cm (6 in) apart each way. One method is to sow several seeds per station, thinning to the strongest. Keep the plants well watered. They will be ready for use within 13–18 weeks. They are a very convenient size for freezing.

Frost protection

Exposed cauliflowers that are maturing in late autumn and very early spring become discoloured and spongy if they thaw out quickly after a frost. Protect the curds either by tying the leaves up above the head or by scooping out a little soil on the north side and gently bending the plant over towards the north.

Pests and diseases

The brassicas are attacked by quite a range of pests and diseases. Watch out for slugs and flea beetle in the early stages and caterpillars, cabbage root fly, aphids and pollen beetle as the plants mature. In recent years cabbage white butterflies have been one of the worst pests: growing the plants under nets is one way of keeping them at bay. The main diseases are club root, downy mildew and leaf spot.

Harvesting

Cut the heads off cauliflowers while they are still firm and before they start to open out.

Use

Preparation for cooking

Trim off coarse outer leaves and cut out any small

Cauliflowers throughout the year

Maturity times may vary according to district; planting distances are given for equal spacing each way.

Group	Sowing	Harvesting	Spacing	Varieties
Spring	late May	Mar–Jun	64 cm (25 in)	Walcheren Winter (Armado April) Vilna
Early summer	early Oct in frames; plant spring	Jun–early Jul	53 cm (21 in)	Montano, Alpha, Paloma
Summer	March	Aug–mid-Sept	53 cm (21 in)	Plana, Dok
Autumn	mid-May	mid-Sept–late Nov	64 cm (25 in)	Plana, White Rock, Canberra, Rosalind, Violet Queen, Romanesco

discoloured patches. A small cauliflower can be cooked whole; make a deep cross in the base so that it cooks evenly. Otherwise break the cauliflower into small branches or segments to cook. Crisp young leaves can also be cooked, and the tender parts of the stem can be cooked or grated raw into salads.

Two methods of protecting cauliflower from frost damage. (Top) Tying up the leaves. (Above) Heeling the plant over to the north, so it will thaw out slowly after frost.

Basic cooking methods

The delicate flavour and crisp texture of cauliflower is easily ruined by overcooking, so boil or steam it until it is only just tender. It can also be stir-fried. After light cooking it can then be baked or fried in egg and breadcrumbs, or used in gratins, curried dishes or salads.

Advice from our expert – *on creating fertile soil rapidly*

Graham Bell adopts the principles of permaculture in his garden, letting nature do as much of the work as possible. 'Sheet mulching' is a method of building up soil fertility on poor ground. It can be used even on the rubble the builders leave behind.

● Start in autumn if possible.
● First cover the ground with cardboard, carpet underlay or carpeting (without foam backing).
● Cover this with a thick layer of compost, leaf mould or manure (it doesn't matter if the latter is fairly raw)
● Cover this with a layer of straw, making the heap at least 15 cm (6 in) high.
● Leave it over the winter, allowing the worms to break it down.
● The following spring it will still be fairly rough, so plant bulky things like potatoes, onion sets, cabbage or spinach plants, or sow large seeds like broad beans.
● By late summer you will have beautiful friable soil. The original cardboard and carpets will have broken down completely.

shoots and stems

By chance, several of the vegetables grown for their shoots are in the luxury class. Asparagus, cardoons and globe artichokes are not only gourmet items on the table but the aristocrats of the kitchen garden, handsome vegetables demanding time and space. Once those demands are met, they are not particularly difficult to grow.

globe artichokes

Globe artichokes thrive in a maritime climate, with warm winters and moist summers. They will not survive severe frost, and must be protected from strong winds. They are perennial plants and, if grown in a suitable climate on fertile, well-drained, moisture-retentive soil can last for many years. The more fertile the soil, the more vigorous and prolific the plants will be. They need a semi-permanent site and, as they are beautiful plants, they are not at all out of place in a flower border.

An artichoke plant normally develops a strong, central primary shoot first, with a large primary artichoke head on the top. After this is picked several smaller secondary heads develop on sideshoots off the main stem; unless it is late in the season they should also reach maturity. A strong plant, generally in its second season, develops a circle of secondary plants around the base of the original stem. Some of these will in time become as strong as the original primary stem, so the plant can end up with three or four primary stems, producing altogether as many as 15 artichoke heads.

Cultivation
Before planting it is essential to work in plenty of well-rotted manure, compost or, if available, seaweed. Once the plants are established maintain fertility by mulching annually with bulky organic manures.

You can start globe artichokes from seed, buy young plants or take offsets (rooted suckers) from established plants.

Raising from seed
Sow in a seed tray indoors in February or outdoors in a seedbed as soon as the soil is workable. Harden off seedlings and plant out in early May. Space the plants at least 90 cm (3 ft) apart each way, and up to 100 cm (4 ft) or more in areas where they thrive. The resulting plants will be very variable in quality, so in their second season propagate from the best plants to increase your stock, and dig up and discard feeble plants.

With their beautiful blue-grey leaves and picturesque flowers buds, globe artichokes will not be out of place in a herbaceous border.

Taking offsets
In mild areas take offsets in autumn; they will start cropping in early summer the following year. In cold areas delay until spring, as offsets may not survive winter. An alternative is to take a few small offsets in autumn, pot them up in large pots, keep them in a greenhouse in winter and plant out in spring.

Prepare the ground for planting by forking the soil deeply and working in well-rotted manure or other organic material. A general fertiliser can also be worked into the soil. Make a hole large enough to take the offsets and plant them slightly below ground level, as the plants have a tendency to work up. Shake the plant as the soil is filled in to prevent the formation of air pockets. If necessary, trim off protruding large roots to fit into the hole; they seem to regrow easily. Water the plant and mulch generously.

In windswept areas, protect offsets with small windbreaks until they are established. A cheap method is to take the bottom out of a net sack and slip it over the plant, keeping it in place with several upright sticks inside the perimeter.

Thinning, replacing, feeding
If plants become very dense cut out a couple of stems so that they remain well ventilated in the centre. As long as plants are growing healthily there is no need to renew them, but if they start to decline in productivity after a few years dig them up and replant offsets. Occasional liquid feeds during growth will be beneficial.

Winter protection
In areas with severe winters, especially if coupled with heavy or poorly drained soil, earth up the base of the plant in early winter and cover it with bracken or litter of some kind. Remove it in spring the following year.

Harvesting
Cut heads with about 15 cm (6 in) of stalk when they are plump. Either cut while they are still tight or wait until they have a little colour and are just starting to open out; some people find the flavour better at this stage. Never wait until the bud leaves harden.

Recommended varieties
In Britain we have little choice so far, but in practice most Continental varieties grow well here. 'Vert de Laon' is best known.

Advice from our expert – on the best way of taking offsets
Tony Lowes, an American now living on the west coast of Ireland, has taken up globe artichokes in a big way. Most gardening books recommend separating off single offsets to establish a new plant, but Tony is convinced it is far better to plant a good section with several young plants together or a main shoot with one or two smaller plants attached. He finds they are stronger and healthier,

producing a much finer crop in their first year. This is how he goes about it:

● Select a fair-sized plant and fork around it, easing it up slightly to see which side will come up with least difficulty.
● Leave the most entrenched third of the plant in place; lift up the remaining two-thirds, cutting it away with a spade.
● Separate this into two parts. The main root system may be very thick and entangled. It can be separated with a spade, but Tony finds there is less damage to the fine fibrous roots if it is sawn through. Keep as much of the original soil on the sections as possible.

Use
Preparation for cooking
Snap off the stem, which pulls away some of the tough fibres in the base of the head. Rub the exposed fleshy rim with lemon juice to prevent it discolouring. (Don't discard the stems as the top 15 cm [6 in] or so are delicious boiled.) Before cooking, pop the heads for a minute or two into water to which vinegar has been added to expel earwigs and other insects hiding in the flowers.

Normally the heads are cooked whole. However, the leaves can be pared off the bases – a somewhat fiddly task – for cooking separately. At every stage of preparation rub exposed surfaces with lemon juice to prevent browning.

Basic cooking methods
Wedge the artichokes upright and boil for 30–50 minutes, depending on size, in water acidulated with the juice of half a lemon or 2 tbsp vinegar per litre (1³/₄ pt). They are ready when the leaves can be pulled off easily or a skewer passed through the whole head. Drain and eat hot or cold. Hot artichokes can be served with melted butter and lemon or a rich hollandaise sauce. Cold artichokes are good with a vinaigrette dressing.

cardoons

Cardoons are perennials in the thistle family. They grow into magnificent plants, their handsome grey leaves spanning an incredible 1.8 m (6 ft), and their flowering spikes towering 2.4 m (8 ft) into the air. They are closely related to globe artichokes, but the leaf stems, rather than the flower buds, are the edible part. The stems are blanched before harvesting to make them tender and less bitter and to bring out their unusual, delicate flavour, somewhat reminiscent of chicory. For culinary

purposes they are best used in their first season, as older plants become tougher and less pliable. They are primarily an early winter and Christmas vegetable.

Cardoons thrive in much the same conditions as globe artichokes, but appear to have more resistance to frost and poor weather. Mature plants are sometimes snapped in half by gales. As with globe artichokes, several types are available on the continent (some more prickly than others) but there is little choice here.

Cultivation
All methods used for cultivating globe artichokes (see p. 29) can be used for cardoons. Prepare the soil as for globe artichokes. Little attention is required during growth other than keeping them weeded, watered, fed and mulched.

Raising from seed
Sow *in situ* in early May, sowing clusters of three or four seeds at intervals about 90 cm (3 ft) apart. Thin to the strongest after germination. Alternatively seeds can be started off indoors, preferably in modules, planting out after hardening off some time in May.

Taking offsets
See globe artichokes. However, cardoons are more vigorous and normally grow well from single offsets.

Blanching
The standard practice on the continent is to start blanching in September, blanching two or three plants a week to get a succession. On a dry day, start by carefully pulling the leaves into an upright position then wrap the stems with any material that will keep out light. Tie it in place if necessary, leaving the leaves protruding from the top. Earth up around the foot of the plant or cover it with straw to keep out light.

Many different materials are used for blanching: heavy brown paper, cardboard, black polythene film, matting, straw, straw plus sacking or black film and so on. In areas with very light soil the stems are sometimes bent over gently and covered with soil to blanch them. Another method is to dig up the entire plant and remove it to the darkness of a shed for blanching.

Harvesting
The stems are normally sufficiently blanched after three to four weeks; they should not be left much longer or they may start to rot. They will also be spoilt by hard frost, so in areas with severe winters blanched plants may be dug up before winter sets in and kept in a cellar or shed until required. (This is quite an operation if the plants are large.)

When the plants are required for eating remove the wrappings and cut off the stems at ground level. They can be left to develop as decorative

plants the following year, but allow at least 1.5 m (5 ft) between plants so they can develop fully.

Advice from our expert – *on preventing bolting*
Clarissa Dickson Wright, who runs the Books for Cooks bookshop in London, has developed an all-consuming passion for this unusual vegetable. Experience has taught her that if cardoons dry out they may simply produce flowers on long stalks without developing succulent leaf stems. Give them a good slosh of water twice a day for the first three weeks and feed once a day. Water normally after that.

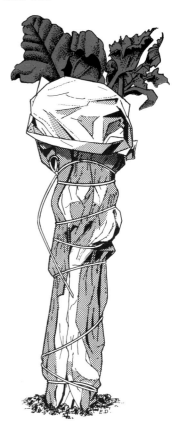

To make them white and tender, the stems of cardoons are blanched by preventing light reaching them. Here they have been tied up with brown paper.

Use
Preparation for cooking
Chop off and discard the leaves and tough outer stems. Slice off any spines along the back of the inner stems and cut the stems into pieces roughly 5 cm (2 in) long. Remove any stringy fibres. Very young, tender stems can be eaten raw.

Basic cooking methods
Start by dropping the pieces into boiling water generously acidulated with lemon juice. Simmer for

10–15 minutes, or until they seem tender and pleasant to taste, then drain. The cooked cardoons can be eaten as they are, reheated in butter, tossed in a well-flavoured vinaigrette to make a salad, stuffed, braised, made into a gratin or served with dips.

asparagus

Asparagus is a perennial crop and, as long as the plants are healthy, beds can remain productive for up to 20 years. The season itself is short, so asparagus can seem an extravagant use of space. Justify it on the grounds that the taste of home-grown asparagus is superb and the fern always looks beautiful. Sow parsley beneath to make better use of the ground.

Asparagus will grow on a wide range of soils; it doesn't require a fertile soil but it does need one that is well-drained and preferably free of stones. It can be grown on the flat or on raised or ridged beds, which improve the drainage and make it easier to produce a whitened stem. Perhaps the easiest way to make a ridge and blanch the stems is to plant on the flat but ridge up later. Never plant on ground that has previously grown asparagus or potatoes as root and nematode infections may develop.

Asparagus naturally produces male and female flowers on separate plants; the female flowers develop into berries. In the old days asparagus beds were a mixture of the two but today there are some all-male F_1 hybrid varieties that are more productive. An even more recent development is of cloned, micro-propagated plants: these are reputed to be twice as productive as the F_1 hybrids. If you are starting from scratch it is worth going for these new varieties.

Cultivation
Dig over the ground the autumn before planting, working in well-rotted farmyard manure or compost. It is absolutely essential to remove all perennial weeds as it is very difficult to weed established asparagus effectively.

You can raise asparagus from seed, or plant one-year-old crowns or young plants raised in modules. Raising from seed is cheapest, but there is an extra year's wait before the first asparagus can be cut.

Raising from seed
It is inadvisable to sow asparagus in its permanent position as there is a high risk of weeds smothering the fragile seedlings. To give plants a good, early start, sow indoors in February at a temperature of 13–16°C (55–60°F). Ideally, sow in modules or small pots, or sow in a seedtray and transplant into modules. Harden off and plant outside in the permanent position in early summer.

An alternative method is to sow in a seedbed outdoors in spring. Thin ordinary seedlings to 5 cm (2 in) apart, and hybrid varieties to 10 cm (4 in) apart. Weed very carefully, cut down any remaining fern in autumn when it has completely died back and mark the rows. Early the following spring (late February or March), before the shoots have appeared, dig up the crowns. They must be handled very carefully, as any damaged roots are easily infected with diseases. For this reason it is advisable to dip the crowns into a fungicide such as Benlate before planting in their permanent position as one-year-old crowns.

Raising from crowns
Plant one-year-old purchased crowns in March or early April. Don't be tempted by two-year-old or three-year-old crowns; the younger ones will get away much better. The average depth for planting asparagus is 13 cm (5 in), but in fact it can be planted as deep as 30 cm (12 in). The deeper the planting, the fewer but larger the spears.

Dig trenches about 30 cm (12 in) wide and the required depth, spacing them 75 cm (2 ft 6 in) apart. Spread out the roots down the centre of each trench and plant them 30–38 cm (12–15 in) apart. If planting at 13 cm (5 in) depth, make the trench 20 cm (8 in) deep, create a little mound of soil about 7.5 cm (3 in) high at the bottom, and spread the crab-like roots over it. Cover the stems with 5 cm (2 in) of fine soil when planting. At the end of the season, cut the stems back when all trace of green has gone, and fill in the soil in the trench. This helps to ensure disease-free plants.

Plants in modules and micro-propagated plants
Plant at the above spacing when you obtain them in spring. Plant at the same depth as crowns, with the roots just covered with soil.

Further care
During the summer weed by hand, or hoe shallowly to avoid damaging the surface roots. Irrigation is very rarely necessary. On windy sites it may be necessary to erect supports around the

plants to prevent them being snapped over. Twine attached to canes works well.

In autumn cut back the dying fern to about 10 cm (4 in) above soil level so the stems are not rocked by the wind. From the second winter onwards, soil can be earthed up around the stems to a height of about 10 cm (4 in) to increase the amount of white stem.

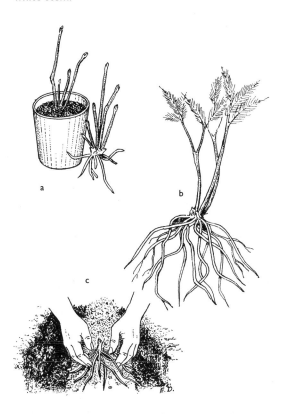

Asparagus can be raised in a number of ways. *(a)* Young, micropropagated plantlets are potted up when received and *(b)* planted out in early summer after hardening off. (c) Planting one-year-old asparagus crowns: the roots are spread over a small mound in the bottom of the trench.

Pests and diseases
During summer watch out for the little beetles and striped larvae of the asparagus beetle on the fern. Squash them or spray with derris.

Harvesting
In most cases harvesting should be delayed until the third season after planting to allow the crowns to build up. A few spears may be cut in their second season from module-raised plants or very vigorous hybrid plants. Cut the buds as they

appear through the soil by inserting a knife about 5 cm (2 in) deep into the soil, taking care not to cut adjacent shoots. Cut for about four weeks in the first season, and six weeks in the following years. If plants are very vigorous, the cutting season can be extended for a couple more weeks. After that, leave the rest of the buds to develop into stems.

Recommended varieties
All-male F₁ hybrids: 'Cito', 'Lucullus', 'Franklym'.
Micro-propagated varieties: 'Sorbonne', 'Versailles'.

Advice from our expert – *on getting the best-flavoured asparagus*
Pete Tomkin has a lifetime's experience and love of asparagus behind him. Although green asparagus is the fashion today he thinks a white stem gives an extra tang, so he mounds up his plants to get that whiteness – and a sprig of mint always goes into the cooking water because it 'gives a little splash of extra flavour'.

Use
Preparation and basic cooking methods
Cut off the earthy lower parts of the stems and tie the asparagus in manageable bundles with string or wide elastic bands. Asparagus is normally either boiled or steamed until tender (but see recipe below) then served with melted butter and black pepper, olive oil or hollandaise sauce. It can also be roasted or grilled. Discarded stems and stringy parts can be used to make soup.

The classic way to cook asparagus
The classic method of cooking asparagus is to partly boil and partly steam it, standing upright with the stems in water in an asparagus steamer. If you don't have one, use the tallest pan you have. Tie the asparagus in bundles and place it upright in the pan, keeping it in place with scrunched-up bundles of silver foil at the base. Pour in water to a depth of 4–5 cm (1½–2 in). Bring the water to the boil, then cover the asparagus with a dome of silver foil to trap the steam. Reduce the heat slightly and cook until the bases are tender. Lift out carefully and drain. If serving it cold run it under the cold tap immediately and drain thoroughly.

salads

Our ancestors were very adventurous with salads. Old garden books record how they mixed commonplace salad plants with wild and cultivated cresses, to which they added nasturtium and primrose flowers, herbs, weeds, buds, cooked and cooled root vegetables and even the seed leaves from sprouted orange and lemon pips. Somewhere along the line that expertise disappeared, and as a result salads have been in the doldrums for the last hundred years or so.

However, there is now a revived interest in inventive salads. The seed catalogues are listing old and new salad plants, some native, some European, even some from the Far East. People are experimenting with sprouted seeds and chicories for mid-winter salads, and it is now fashionable to use edible wild plants and edible flowers for spice and colour. Although some unusual salad items can be found in good greengrocers and supermarkets, gardeners have a great advantage as it is very easy to grow something different for the salad bowl.

radishes

Almost every kitchen plot grows a few of the typical small summer radishes, whose roots can be long or round and red, pink, white or bicoloured. These are the fastest maturing and easiest to grow. For the salad specialist there are large-rooted radishes, plus radish leaves, seed pods and sprouted seeds.

Large-rooted radishes
Mooli or daikon
These Eastern radishes are usually white-skinned and white-fleshed. They are often 25 cm (10 in) long, and 4 cm (1½ in) in diameter. The varieties currently available are at their best from late summer to autumn.

Beauty Heart radish
This is a magnificent radish from North China. From the outside it looks like a large round turnip but the inside of a good specimen is a brilliant pink, with a sweet flavour and juicy texture. The new variety 'Mantanghong' has been developed for British growing conditions.

Winter radish
These rather coarse, relatively hardy radishes are round or long, with black, violet, red or pink skins. In most parts of the country they can be left in the ground during winter or lifted and stored like carrots.

Cultivation
All radishes grow best on light, well-drained soil. They are not very greedy plants but they do need a constant supply of moisture throughout growth or their quality deteriorates. Ordinary radishes can be intersown between slow-growing vegetables to make the best use of garden space. They can also be mixed with the seed of slow-growing vegetables like parsnips or carrots and sown together so that the faster-growing radishes will mark the rows, which can then be hoed without damaging the seedlings that are on their way up. In the early stages flea beetle can be a serious problem.

Ordinary radishes
Sow in situ from early spring until late summer in shallow drills 13 mm (½ in) deep and 15 cm (6 in) apart. Try to sow very thinly, spacing seeds 2.5 cm (1 in) apart, so there will be no need to thin any further; otherwise you will have to thin them out, as radishes never develop well once they have become crowded.

Radishes are normally ready within three to four weeks. The secret of success is sowing little and often. For a continuous supply sow in succession: as soon as one lot is through the soil, sow the next. Early spring and autumn sowings can be made under cover.

Pull the roots as they reach the required size. Never leave them too long as most varieties become spongy or tough with age.

There's more to radishes than we might think: *(a)* large mooli radish, *(b)* pink-fleshed 'Beauty Heart' radish, *(c)* 'Bisai' radish grown for its leaves, *(d)* common small radish, *(e & f)* radish seed pods, *(g)* sprouted radish seeds.

Mooli radish
Many mooli varieties have a tendency to bolt without developing roots if sown early; to be on the safe side, sow *in situ* from June to the end of August. Sow about 1 cm ('/₂ in) deep in rows at least 30 cm (12 in) apart, thinning to 10–20 cm (4–8 in) apart, depending on variety. They are normally ready for use in about eight weeks. Once ready, they need to be used fairly soon.

Mooli are susceptible to flea beetle and cabbage root fly. Growing them under fine nets protects them from these pests.

Beauty Heart radish
Sow the variety 'Mantanghong' *in situ* outdoors from late May until July. Sow about 1cm ('/₂ in) deep and 20 cm (8 in) apart each way. For a slightly earlier crop, sow indoors in modules in April. Harden off and transplant outside when the seedlings have three to five true leaves. If you want Beauty Heart radish at Christmas, sow in modules in late August and transplant them to an unheated greenhouse or polytunnel. Beauty Heart radish matures in 10–12 weeks, and will remain in good condition for several weeks without deteriorating. It is attacked by the same pests as mooli radish.

Large winter radish
Sow *in situ* in July and August as for mooli radish, thinning to 23 cm (9 in) apart each way. In most areas they can be left in the ground for winter, covered with a thick layer of straw. In very severe areas lift them in winter and store them in a shed in boxes of moist sand or ashes.

Radish seed pods
When radishes bolt they produce flowers which develop into small pods. If picked while still young and green these pods are very succulent. The flavour varies from faintly radishy to quite hot, depending on the variety. 'Munchen Bier' is especially recommended for this purpose. The large winter radishes also produce excellent pods – just leave a plant in the soil in spring so that it will run to seed naturally. In fact, any radish can be left to run to seed for its pods, but on the whole the larger the radish the larger and more succulent the pods will be. It is then a case of trial and error to see which have the most likeable flavour. Pick the pods frequently to encourage more to develop.

Radish leaves
Young radish leaves can be very tasty raw, while older leaves can be cooked like greens. In the old days radishes were broadcast in hotbeds in winter to get very early spring crops of tender little leaves. Most small radishes have leaves that are tender when young. Sow fairly thickly, or broadcast in wide drills (see oriental greens, p. 25), and cut them off about 1 cm ('/₂ in) above soil level. They will often resprout.

The newly introduced Japanese variety 'Bisai' has been bred especially for its leaves. It can be sown any time from early spring to autumn, and is often ready for cutting within three weeks. If the plants are left to grow larger the leaves become coarser, but can still be cooked. If the plants are eventually thinned to about 10 cm (4 in) apart, fairly large roots like those of mooli will develop. Early and late sowings can be made under cover.

Radish sprouts

Radish seeds can be sprouted like mustard and cress on moist flannel or blotting paper or in a seed sprouter or jar. They can be eaten within a few days when 1–2 cm ($^1/_2$–$^3/_4$ in) long and have a very pleasant flavour. Fast-germinating types like 'Bisai' are recommended.

Recommended varieties

Ordinary radishes: 'French Breakfast', 'Parat', '18-day', 'Red Prince'. Mooli radish: 'April Cross', 'Mino Early', 'Minowase Summer Cross'. Beauty Heart radish: 'Mantanghong'. Large winter radish: 'Black Spanish Round', 'Cherokee', 'China Rose'. Radish seed pods: 'Munchen Bier'. Radish leaves and sprouts: 'Bisai'.

Advice from our expert – *on keeping radishes succulent*

Adrian Jones grows an amazing range of radishes on his allotment, but whatever the type, he says, 'It's a steady supply of water that's the most important thing for succulent radishes.' That steady supply prevents them running to seed and becoming hard and pithy.

Use

Small radishes, young seedling leaves, seed pods and sprouted seeds are usually eaten raw in salads. Wash if necessary and chill before serving.

Large radishes can be sliced or grated into salads. If the flavour is very hot peel them, as the 'heat' is usually in the skin. They can also be cut into pieces and boiled, added to stews, roasted under a joint, or glazed in a pan with butter and sugar.

Seed pods and sprouted seeds can be lightly stir-fried as well as being eaten raw, and the larger radish leaves can be cooked briefly like spinach.

---

exotic salads

The dedicated salad-lover wants to be able to pick fresh, interesting salads from the garden all year round. It is surprisingly easy to accomplish this, even in very small gardens – you just need to take an adventurous approach. This begins with a willingness to use unusual plants or different parts of familiar plants, such as the flowers of nasturtium and chives and the seed pods of radishes. Next step is to adopt different growing and harvesting methods, such as 'cut-and-come again'. This is a wonderful way of growing delicious, almost instant seedlings for salads or of prolonging the cutting of lettuces, oriental greens and many other plants.

The third step is the use of protection – growing under cover. With a bit of shelter, the quality of salad plants and the range that can be grown is increased dramatically both in the autumn to spring period and, in cold and exposed areas, in summer.

Composing salads

The secret of lively salads is a harmonious mixture of salad plants. Our salad expert, Frances Smith, starts with a base of crunchy, well-flavoured lettuce and adds a few leaves with interesting textures, a smattering of stronger or sharp-flavoured leaves and something novel or colourful, such as flowers or mangetout pea pods. Even very sharp leaves become modified if shredded, dressed and mixed with blander salad plants. Here are some ideas for salad plants that are a little different. Use the 'Salad Calendar' as a starting point for planning a year-round salad garden.

Lettuces

For crunchy flavour 'Little Gem' takes some beating. Bronze-tinged varieties such as 'Marvel of Four Seasons' have a good flavour. The 'Salad Bowl' types are very pretty in both their red and green forms; they don't form hearts and can be picked leaf by leaf over a long period. 'Red Lollo' and 'Green Lollo' are particularly decorative. Watch out for some dramatic red lettuces appearing in seed catalogues.

Traditional salad plants

Many old-fashioned plants are perfect in salads. For sharp flavours grow sorrel, land cress, chicories, endives and salad rocket (not to be confused with the flower sweet rocket). For something milder try the green and yellow forms of summer purslane and the gentle but very hardy corn salad (also known as lamb's lettuce or mache).

Introductions from abroad

The sparkling Mediterranean iceplant (*Mesembryanthemum crystallinum*) makes the most picturesque summer salad, while the American winter purslane or claytonia is at its best in autumn and spring. Most of the new oriental greens and radishes can be used in salads (see pp. 24–26 and 34).

Edible weeds and wild plants

A surprising number of weeds and wild plants are edible, but do check their identity if you are unsure of them. Dandelion, chickweed, shepherd's purse, jack-by-the-hedge, ground elder, fat hen and hairy bittercress are some common weeds and hedgerow plants that are edible and have a lovely taste. Always pick young small leaves; older leaves quickly become coarse and tough.

Herbs

Herbs can transform salads, but they should always be used very sparingly. Variegated and coloured forms of mints, marjoram and thyme add taste, texture and brightness; bronze and green fennel have wonderful texture; garlic chives gives a hint of garlic and rubbing a bowl with lovage bestows a unique celery flavour. Try chervil for an aniseed touch. In fact, experiment with any herbs in the garden: most can find a place in a salad.

Edible flowers

Many garden flowers are edible. A few have a distinct taste, but most are included simply for their colour. Add them to a salad after it has been tossed. Petalled flowers like daisies and pot marigolds can be pulled apart and sprinkled over the top like confetti. Roses, borage, violets, pansies, nasturtiums (both petals and leaves are edible, with a peppery flavour), day lilies and chive flowers are among the best to use.

Cut-and-come-again methods
Salad seedlings

Many plants can be grown as salad seedlings, cut at 5–10 cm (2–4 in) high when they are at their most tender, tasty and nutritious. They are very productive, because they can be grown in small spaces or even in containers. The first cuts can be made anything from two to four weeks after sowing, depending on the time of year. Simply cut with scissors or a penknife, about 1 cm (³/₄ in) above the soil. In many cases the seedlings will resprout to give a second or third cut a couple of weeks later.

Salad seedling sowings can be made all year round, but will run to seed faster in hot weather. Sow broadcast, in rows or, preferably, in wide flat drills (see oriental greens, p. 25). Very useful early and late sowings can be made under cover.

Some of the best salads to grow as seedlings include ordinary garden cress, salad rape (which is mild-flavoured and long-lasting), salad mustard, rocket, summer and winter purslane, oriental greens (especially pak choi, mizuna, komatsuna and Oriental Saladini), 'Salad Bowl' types of lettuce, curly endive, 'Bisai' radish and Texsel greens.

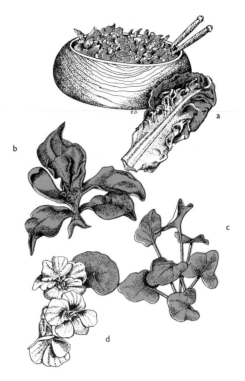

The harmonious mixture of a composed salad: *(a)* crunchy, well-flavoured 'Little Gem' lettuce, *(b)* iceplant with its interesting texture, *(c)* lemon-flavoured buckler-leaved sorrel, and *(d)* nasturtium flowers for colour.

Cutting mature plants

The harvesting season for many salad plants can be prolonged by either picking a few leaves at a time or by cutting across the plant rather than uprooting it. In both cases the plants produce more leaves. 'Salad Bowl' lettuces, chicories and endives, all the purslanes, corn salad, rocket, fennel, the oriental greens and many others respond well to this treatment; see under 'Semi-mature harvesting' in the section on oriental greens on page 25 for more details. It is worth experimenting with any salad plants in the garden to see which can be coaxed into producing more leaf.

Protection

It is amazing what a little protection does for salad plants; just being sheltered from winds makes them infinitely more tender and far more productive. In winter it often makes the difference between life and death, because it is the deadly combination of wind and low temperature which kills plants.

Greenhouses (they don't need to be heated) and walk-in polytunnels are the most luxurious forms of protection for salad crops. They can be planted up in autumn with endives, chicories, oriental greens, winter lettuce and so on, or sown with seedling salads. Next best are garden frames and cloches. If you have none of these, rig up low polythene film tunnels over salad plants or cover them with fleecy films during the winter months.

Harvesting and use

The joy of home-grown salads is having them fresh: nothing deteriorates as fast as salads. Pick them early in the day while still fresh. Handle leaves very gently to avoid bruising them and lay them flat in a basket or, in hot weather, pop them straight into a plastic bag. If they are soiled wash them carefully in a large bowl of water, drain and pat dry in a tea towel. Toss them in a dressing just before serving.

Advice from our expert – *on finding, and keeping, unusual salad seed*

Frances Smith and her husband grow exotic salads for restaurants, and hunt down interesting seed abroad where the choice is wider. (There's normally no problem in bringing packeted seed into the country.) Seed keeps best in cool, dry conditions so Frances suggests keeping precious seed in an airtight jar at the back of the fridge.

Salad Calendar				
	Spring	**Summer**	**Autumn**	**Winter**
Lettuce base	Little Gem Winter Density Salad Bowl	Little Gem Salad Bowl	Little Gem Salad Bowl	Winter Density Salad Bowl
For sharp flavour	Sorrel Cress Rocket Sugar loaf chicory	Sorrel Rocket Endive Sugar loaf chicory	Sorrel Cress Rocket Sugar loaf chicory	Sorrel Rocket Land cress Sugar loaf chicory
For texture	Winter purslane Witloof chicory Oriental greens	Summer purslane Iceplant Fennel	Corn salad Winter purslane Oriental greens	Corn salad Oriental greens Witloof chicory
For colour or novelty	Red chicory Radish seed pods Hairy bittercress Winter pansies Daisies Chinese chives	Mangetout peas Bronze fennel Yellow tomatoes Borage Nasturtium Pot marigold Radish seed pods Fat hen	Red chicory Beauty Heart radish Chinese chive flowers Hairy bittercress	Red chicory Ornamental kale Red mustard Winter pansies

red and Witloof chicory

The chicories are typical of vegetables that are very popular on the continent, especially in Italy, but relatively unknown here. There are many types, all of which are easily grown and tolerant of a wide range of soils and conditions. In varying degrees they all have a slightly bitter flavour (even the blue flowers), and this may be why they have never taken off here. However, the bitterness can be masked by shredding the leaves, by mixing them with other salad plants and by blanching them in the dark.

Here we look at two types: red chicory, often known as radicchio (the Italian name for chicory) and Witloof or Belgian chicory, which is forced to produce a white 'chicon'.

red chicory

The red chicories have highly coloured leaves, ranging from varieties with yellowish speckled leaves to those which are deep red. Some are green initially, only turning red in the autumn. Most types are an untidy rosette at first, but as the season progresses the leaves gradually curl inwards to form a rounded, blanched heart. These beautiful inner leaves are whitish pink, crisp, and much sweeter than the outer leaves. 'Red Treviso' has long leaves and never forms a heart, but it can be blanched like Witloof chicory to make a stunning white chicon with a pinkish tinge. The range of varieties has increased in the last few years and, with the introduction of hybrid varieties, the quality has also improved. In the past getting a good chicory head was quite a gamble.

Chicories vary in hardiness, but only 'Red Treviso' types survive outdoors every winter. Others can be grown outdoors until late autumn, then protected with cloches to prolong the season. They can also be grown in unheated greenhouses in winter.

Cultivation
Chicories can be sown *in situ* in rows about 30 cm (12 in) apart, thinning to 20–35 (8–14 in) apart, depending on the variety. Chicory can also be sown in seedtrays or modules and transplanted outside when it has several leaves. It tolerates some shade, so can be planted among other plants if space is short.

Sow early varieties in late April and May – these will mature during the summer. Continue sowing later varieties in June and early July for autumn heads. Finally, sow a few plants in late July and transplant them into greenhouses or polytunnels in late August for a winter crop.

Very little attention is required during the summer months. Chicory is rarely seriously attacked by pests and, provided the soil is reasonably fertile and moisture retentive, rarely requires extra watering. In late autumn protect any remaining plants with cloches, low polythene film tunnels or fleece. Plants are sometimes covered by straw for the winter. They remain in good condition beneath it, but there is a risk of it attracting mice or even rats.

Harvesting
For salad, wait until a tight heart has formed before cutting the plant; some of the outer leaves can be picked sooner for garnishing. Cut across

the heart, but don't uproot the plant as it may continue sprouting over many more months. Plants that are cut in the autumn may remain virtually dormant in winter and if not killed by frost will start growing again in spring, producing more usable leaves.

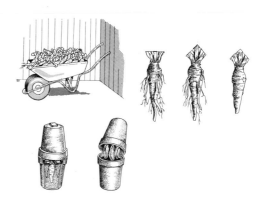

The stages in forcing Witloof chicory : (top left) allowing the roots to wilt after lifting; *(top right)* trimming off wispy roots and cutting the top into a conical shape; *(lower left)* potting up the roots in a pot, which is covered with a pot of the same size with the drainage hole blocked; *(lower right)* mature chicons.

The natural 'Red Treviso' leaves can be used throughout the winter, but they are much more tender if blanched. Follow the same procedure as for Witloof chicory, but don't expect the chicons to be as substantial.

In late spring, chicory leaves become very coarse and the plants run to seed, producing beautiful flowering spikes up to 1.8 m (6 ft) high which are covered in masses of blue flowers that close at midday. Use them in salads.

Recommended varieties
For early sowings: 'Alouette', 'Cesare', 'Rossano'. For late sowings: 'Red Devil', 'Red Treviso', 'Verona Palla Rossa'.

Use
Red chicory is mainly used raw for garnishing and in salads to add colour and a crunchy texture. The flavour is subtly changed by cooking, which, sadly, destroys the colour. Red chicory can be braised, brushed with olive oil and grilled, or used in any recipes for Witloof chicory.

Witloof chicory

The cultivation of Witloof chicory falls into two phases: growing it in summer, then lifting it and forcing it in the dark in winter. As with red chicory, the recently introduced F$_1$ hybrid varieties are much more reliable and easy to force than old-fashioned varieties.

Sow Witloof like red chicory *in situ* in May, thinning

the plants to about 23 cm (9 in) apart. Other than weeding and watering if necessary to prevent the soil drying out completely, no attention is needed. The plants look like large dandelions, and indeed are closely related.

Dig out the roots any time from late October to December. After lifting leave them outside, sheltered from the rain, for up to two weeks. This is to check the growth and allow moisture to pass back into the roots. Then trim off the leaves about 2.5 cm (1 in) above the neck; these can be eaten but are generally a bit coarse and bitter. Reject any roots that are less than 4 cm (1½ in) in diameter across the top. Store the roots until required for forcing. Lay them horizontally in boxes of peat or sand in a shed or in a 30 cm (12 in) deep trench in the garden. For a regular supply of Witloof chicory during the winter months it is only necessary to lift and force a few at a time.

Forcing the roots
The simplest way to force roots is to plant them up in soil in flower pots of about 23 cm (9 in) in diameter. Select three to five roots of roughly the same size, trim off odd pieces of root that are jutting out and trim off wispy lower roots so they will fit neatly into the pot. They need to be planted close but not touching, with the necks about 2.5 cm (1 in) out of the soil. Pack soil around them and shake it down. It doesn't matter what type soil you use; it is only there to keep the roots upright and prevent them drying out. The chicons get all their nourishment from the roots. After planting, cover the pot with an identical upturned pot. Block any drainage holes with tinfoil or a stone to keep out the light. Water lightly.

The roots need to be forced in darkness at a temperature of 10–18°C (50–64°F). An airing cupboard, provided it is not too hot, is an ideal place. At 18°C (64°F) it takes about three weeks for the chicons to develop. Inspect the plants occasionally to make sure there are no signs of rotting, and water lightly if they are drying out.

Harvesting
When the chicons are nice and plump cut them about 2 cm (¾ in) above the root. Leave the root as it will probably produce a second flush of little leaves. Keep the chicons wrapped in brown paper in the fridge, as any exposure to light turns them green and they become bitter-tasting again.

Recommended varieties
Hybrids 'Zoom' and 'Normato'.

Advice from our expert – *on encouraging a well-shaped chicon*
Ned Trier has a flourishing vegetable garden and loves the chicories. When cutting the leaves for forcing, he recommends cutting upwards to make a little pointed crown in the centre. This safeguards the growing point, and allows any moisture to drain away.

Use
Preparation for cooking
For use raw in salads simply strip off individual leaves, clean them if necessary, and slice them or use them whole.

Basic cooking method
Cooking gives chicory a distinctive and unusual flavour. The chicons can be braised, steamed, simmered in water to which lemon has been added, glazed and used in various dishes.

Witloof chicory with Roquefort cheese
Serves 4–6 as an hors d'oeuvre

3 heads of chicory

For the dressing:
40 g (1½ oz) Roquefort or Cabrales cheese
75 ml / 5 tbsp mayonnaise
30–45 ml / 2–3 tbsp milk
squeeze of lemon
2 tbsp chopped fresh parsley
cayenne pepper

Either quarter the chicory heads lengthwise or separate them into individual leaves. Arrange on a serving plate and cover.
Mash the cheese to a paste and then beat in the mayonnaise, followed by the milk. Stir in the lemon juice, parsley and cayenne pepper. Taste and adjust seasonings, adding more lemon juice or cayenne if you think it needs it. Spoon over the quartered chicory. If you have separated out the leaves, place a dessertspoonful of dressing in the curve of each leaf at the widest end.

---

fruiting vegetables

The fruiting vegetables – tomatoes, peppers and aubergines – are gourmet luxuries from the garden and are among the most rewarding to grow. A freshly picked, home-grown tomato is a world apart from a shop-bought one. All originate in warm climates, and growing superbly flavoured tomatoes and the closely related peppers and aubergines presents something of a challenge in our cool islands.

tomatoes

Terry Marshall is the committed organic gardener whose Yorkshire garden and allotment were visited for the *Grow Your Greens, Eat Your Greens* tomato programme. He has over 40 years' experience of tomato-growing, both professionally and at home, and is constantly experimenting with ways of growing tomatoes without using chemicals. Here are his thoughts on some aspects of growing tomatoes organically in greenhouses.

Climate

Tomatoes are tender plants that are damaged by frost, so they only grow outdoors successfully in warm areas or on sheltered sites. To work out what the odds are on success in your area, find out the likely dates of the last spring frost and the first autumn frost and see if that will provide the eight weeks it takes an average tomato to go from flowering to fruiting. (They are normally planted out at the flowering stage.) If the answer is no, it is better to grow tomatoes in cold frames, unheated polytunnels or a greenhouse.

Greenhouse design and hygiene

In northern latitudes the poor light as much as low temperatures makes it hard to get tomatoes off to an early start. To make the most of winter light, Terry built his greenhouse against a south-facing wall (which retains heat) with the glass on the south, west and east sides angled at 60 degrees. This allows the low winter light to penetrate rather than being reflected off as happens with vertical glass.

To combat the very high temperatures which then occur in summer, Terry has devised several means of ventilation. Air comes in through hollow wall blocks laid horizontally beneath the glass and along the top of the wall. Corner pieces of glass have been dry-glazed, and these can be removed in June or July to provide a cross-current of air. Two automatic vents open in very hot weather. To Terry, a good flow of air is one key to keeping plants disease-free and is easier than shading the greenhouse.

Another means of combating pests and diseases is keeping the greenhouse spotlessly clean. Terry scrubs it completely with liquid soap at the end of each season. Any diseased material is cleared out as soon as it appears and no diseased plants are ever brought in.

Preparing the greenhouse soil

If tomatoes are grown for several years in the same soil, diseases develop. The soil then has to be changed, or the tomatoes grown in containers. One advantage of polytunnels is that they can easily be moved to a fresh site after a few years if the soil is diseased. There are also some disease-resistant varieties of tomatoes, or tomatoes can be grafted on to disease-resistant rootstocks to overcome the problem.

Terry prepares the greenhouse soil very thoroughly by digging a trench, breaking up the subsoil and, as he works across the area, working in manure and compost. Three weeks before planting he works an organic base dressing consisting of fine hoof and horn, fine bonemeal, seaweed meal and calcified seaweed in equal measures into the top 23 cm (9 in) of soil at the rate of 250 g/sq m (8 oz/sq yd).

Sowing

Tomatoes are planted out six to eight weeks after sowing. Sowing in late February/early March is early enough in most areas for indoor tomatoes. Terry sows in seed compost he makes from a 50:50 mixture of sieved leaf mould and sharp sand. Seeds are spaced 5 cm (2 in) apart in a seed tray, and put to germinate in a propagator in the dark. The ideal germination temperature is 20°C (68°F), but anything from 15–21°C (60–70°F) is acceptable. Use the airing cupboard if necessary.

As soon as the seedlings germinate move them into good light, and try to keep them at about 18°C (65°F) during the day and 13°C (55°F) at night. When the leaves of adjacent plants are touching pot them on into about 11 cm (4 $\frac{1}{2}$ in) pots. Terry has developed his own comfrey compost for the purpose. It is quite easy to make your own.

Comfrey compost

First grow your comfrey. Start with bought-in plants, or rooted offsets taken from established plants. The 'Bocking 14' strain is the most productive. Plant them 60–90 cm (2–3 ft) apart any time from spring to autumn. Remove the flowering shoot in the first growing season and start cutting leaves from the second season. Cut several times a year, 5 cm (2 in) above ground level, when the plants are 60 cm (2 ft) high. Comfrey plants last many years, provided they are watered in dry seasons and manured regularly. You need roughly twice as many comfrey plants as tomato plants if you want to produce sufficient compost.

Then make your leaf mould. Collect up all your leaves in autumn and keep them in a heap enclosed by wire netting. Where practical, make a separate heap of tougher, slightly richer leaves like beech and oak. Leave the heaps for at least 18 months to rot down naturally into leaf mould.

Make the compost in September when the potash levels are highest in the comfrey leaves. Take a strong plastic sack and line the bottom with a layer of leaf mould roughly 7.5 cm (3 in) deep. (If you have two types, mix them together.) Cover this with a similar layer of comfrey leaves, lightly pressing them down. Alternate leaf mould and comfrey layers until the sack is full.

Tie the sack at the neck or bend the plastic over and weight it down with a brick. Make some ventilation holes with a garden fork and leave it in a sheltered spot. It will be ready for use the following spring.

Planting

After potting keep the plants in good light, moving them further and further apart as they grow so they are never crowded. (This is another of Terry's secrets of success.) Water them so they are just moist, but not wet. When the first flowers are showing plant them in the soil, or into growing bags or large pots at least 25–30 cm (10–12 in) in diameter. Fill the pots with comfrey compost mixed with Terry's organic base dressing above.

Space the tomato plants about 45 cm (18 in) apart. They will need supports, the simplest being strings suspended from wires running along the top of the greenhouse. Attach the strings below the lowest leaves and twist the tomato stems around them as they grow, at the same time nipping out the sideshoots. Towards the end of July or in early August 'stop' them by nipping out the top growing point a couple of leaves beyond the top truss. This will allow time for the remaining tomatoes to mature before the end of October.

De-leafing and mulching

The lower leaves on the stems will gradually turn yellow and lose their synthesising power. Cut them off in stages with a sharp knife so as to improve the air circulation among the plants, which will help to keep them healthy. Remove only those leaves below a fruiting truss; leave any that are near the glass or are sheltering a truss.

After de-leafing, the roots are more exposed to sun and may become dried out, so it is a good time to mulch them with up to 5 cm (2 in) of garden compost or chopped comfrey stems.

Watering and feeding

In the early stages plants need about 150 ml ($\frac{1}{4}$ pt) of water a week, increasing to as much as 1–1.7 litres ($1\frac{3}{4}$–3 pt) a day in mid-season. Once fruits start to set Terry waters roughly three times a week with comfrey liquid. After the third truss has formed he also waters every 10 days or so with liquid seaweed, which helps to stimulate new roots. The leaves get a foliar spray of liquid seaweed roughly every 10 days in order to prevent trace element deficiencies and to make the leaves tougher and more disease-resistant. If plants look pale later in the season he waters them with liquid poultry manure, made by suspending a sack of chicken manure in a barrel of water.

Pollination

Tomatoes are normally self-pollinating, but in very hot and dry conditions pollen may be killed off. To encourage pollination, first sprinkle the greenhouse lightly with water to increase the humidity. Come back an hour later and tap the wires to distribute the pollen.

Damping down

Sprinkling the greenhouse with water when temperatures are high is always a good practice. It lowers the temperature and so discourages pests like red spider mite which thrive at high temperatures.

Comfrey concentrate

Make comfrey concentrate in a plastic barrel with a hole drilled in the bottom. (Terry screws an old tap into his barrels). Stand the barrel on bricks with a jar or pot under the hole. Stuff the barrel with comfrey leaves, cover them with a board and weight them down. Concentrated juice will start dripping through within two weeks. Dilute it 10–20 times with water before use. Keep putting more comfrey leaves into the barrel to maintain the supply.

Flavour
Tomato flavour varies according to the season, the variety and the growing methods. Underwatered tomatoes have more flavour than well-watered, and comfrey compost may increase flavour. Tomatoes have sweet and acid elements, the sweet originating in the outer flesh, the acid in the juicy central pulp. Some varieties are more acid if picked slightly early. Experiment with varieties and the stage of picking to see what appeals to your taste buds.

Recommended varieties
'Abunda', very reliable, early fruiting with excellent flavour; 'Ailsa Craig', old-fashioned but still among best-flavoured; 'Gardener's Delight', small, sweet, cherry tomatoes; vigorous and easy to grow; 'Shirley', modern variety with excellent disease resistance; 'Sioux', juicy, rich-coloured fruits of variable size but excellent flavour; 'Sungold', a new variety with exceptionally sweet, golden-skinned, cherry-size fruits and vigorous plants; 'Supermarmande', large Continental type with excellent flavour and texture; 'Tumbler', prolific cascading variety recommended for hanging baskets and tubs.

Hanging growing-bag panniers
Terry makes a decorative feature of tomatoes using the cascading variety 'Tumbler' (see

illustrations below). Pick up an unopened growing bag by the middle, shake the contents so they divide evenly between the two halves (a), and place it over a tree branch, fence or rail (b) in a sheltered but sunny position. Make a slit on each side (c), about 7.5 cm (3 in) below the centre, and plant two 'Tumbler' tomatoes on each side through the slit. It will be cascading with tomatoes by the end of the season (d).

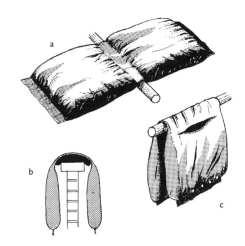

Use
Besides being eaten fresh, tomatoes can be baked, stuffed, fried and used in soups, sauces, casseroles and stews and a great variety of other dishes. To preserve them for winter, freeze them (the English-bred 'Britain's Breakfast' freezes beautifully), make them into tomato purée or bottle them. To skin tomatoes, cover with boiling water and leave for a couple of minutes. The skin then peels off easily.

---

peppers

Peppers grow on fairly compact bushes, and are cultivated much like tomatoes. They need good light and reasonable warmth, so in cold parts of the country grow them in unheated greenhouses or cold frames in the soil, in growing bags or in 20–25 cm (8–10 in) pots. In warm areas they can be grown in a sheltered spot outdoors.

There are two main types of pepper. The plump sweet peppers known as capsicums are green when immature, ripening in warm conditions to yellow, orange, red or violet black. The much hotter chilli types are often long and thin; green when immature, they ripen to red or yellow. However, both types come in all colours, sizes and shapes. Sweet peppers get sweeter as they colour, hot peppers get hotter. The hybrid varieties bred for cool climates are the easiest to grow. Dwarf varieties are recommended for window-boxes and small containers.

Cultivation

Prepare the soil by working in plenty of well-rotted organic matter, preferably the previous autumn. A base dressing can be worked in before planting.

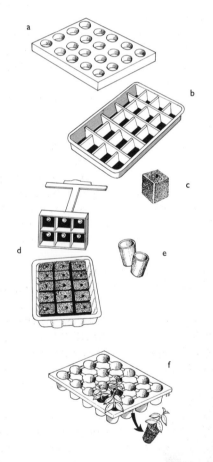

Different types of modules: (a) polystyrene tray, (b) divided seed tray, (c) soil block, (d) Ladbrooke miniblocker, (e) pots, (f) PG Quick-pot propagation tray with pepper ready for planting.

Sow in mid-March in seedtrays at a temperature of about 21°C (70°F). When the seedlings are about 2.5 cm (1 in) high, prick them out into 5–7.5 cm (2–3 in) pots. They can be potted on again into 10–13 cm (4–5 in) pots if you want extra-strong

plants. Plant them in their permanent positions, in the soil or in containers, when about 11 cm (4½ in) high, with the flowers just showing. Harden them off very well beforehand and give them extra protection on cold nights with cloches or fleecy films. Don't plant outside until all risk of frost is past. Average spacing is 40 cm (16 in) apart, but dwarf varieties and chillies can be 30 cm (12 in) apart. Peppers don't usually require supports.

Misting

Peppers benefit from relatively high humidity, especially in hot weather. To create a moist tropical micro-climate around his peppers, our pepper expert Nevel Vassel sprays them gently with water every morning during hot weather. They can be 'damped down' again at midday. This helps fruits to set, stops buds dropping off, and discourages red spider mite. Buckets of water placed throughout the greenhouse also help to create humidity.

Feeding, watering and mulching

Once the pepper fruits have started to form the plants may benefit from extra feeding. Feed them every 10 days or so with a general-purpose or seaweed-based fertiliser. If the plants seem very healthy and are growing vigorously, feeding may not be necessary; peppers are less demanding than tomatoes in this respect. Water enough to prevent the soil drying out. Mulch the plants, especially when grown indoors, to keep the soil pleasantly moist.

Pests and diseases

Outdoor peppers have few problems other than cold weather and are usually disease-free. The most common pests indoors are whitefly, aphids and red spider mite.

Harvesting and storage

The first peppers are ready roughly 13 weeks after sowing. They take another four to six weeks to develop their mature colour, so in a poor English summer only early and mid-season peppers will mature. Green peppers can be picked as soon as they are smooth and glossy.

Peppers continue to develop surprisingly late in the autumn, but if frost is threatened protect them at night with fleecy films or cloches. At the end of the season, before they are damaged by frost, pull the plants up by their roots and hang them in a sunny porch. The remaining fruits will gradually change colour and will keep in reasonable condition for several weeks. Chilli peppers will dry on the plant, and can be kept this way for up to two years. Alternatively, store them in jars once fully dried.

Recommended varieties
Early-maturing hybrids: 'Bell Boy', 'Early Prolific', 'Ace'. Dwarf forms: 'Red Skin', 'Apache' (chilli). Recommended for flavour: 'Hungarian Wax' (sweet in its early stages, hot when mature).

Advice from our expert – *on the perfect sowing compost for peppers and on saving the seed of 'Scotch Bonnets'*
Nevel Vassel was brought up in Jamaica and now runs the horticultural department at Bilston Community College. To give peppers the best possible start he sows them in general-purpose sowing and potting compost, sieving it carefully first to remove any fibrous material. Seeds germinate beautifully in the resulting fine compost.

Nevel loves the wrinkled, hot, West Indian 'Scotch Bonnet' pepper, but seed is hard to get here unless you buy the peppers at a West Indian grocery or market stall. You can save the seeds of bought peppers in this manner: first dip the pepper in a fungicide such as Benlate, then put it on a sunny windowsill until dry. When dry, split it open, take out the seeds and spread them out on a paper to dry further. Store them in envelopes in a cool, dry place.

Use
Preparation for cooking
Many recipes require peppers to be skinned before cooking. The simplest method of doing this is to put them under the grill until blackened then peel off the loosened skin. Grilled peppers are excellent cold in salad.

Basic methods of cooking
Peppers can be worked into all sorts of dishes, as well as being fried, braised or stuffed and baked. If you are stuffing them blanch them briefly first in boiling water. They are also lovely raw in salads.

aubergines

Aubergines are often twinned with peppers because they are grown in the same way. However, they are trickier than peppers, needing slightly higher temperatures and more fertile soil. They are also more likely to go down suddenly with pests or disease.

In comparison with peppers, there is a smaller choice of varieties bred for chilly climates like ours. The large purple-fruited type is the main one grown, but there is also a pretty, white-skinned, egg-shaped variety on the market. Smaller-fruited ones and long, thin types are also sometimes available in seed catalogues.

Cultivation
Follow instructions for peppers (see p. 44). Once the seedlings have germinated try to maintain a minimum temperature of 16°C (60°F) at night and 18°C (64°F) during the day. Aubergines grow into bushier plants than peppers, so can be spaced about 45 cm (18 in) apart. Mulch them after planting to keep the roots cool.

Aubergines require quite a lot of watering in dry weather. Once the fruits are starting to set, plants can be fed with a tomato fertiliser every 10 days or so. In addition damp down the greenhouse regularly as for peppers.

Harvesting
Aubergines can be picked at any stage. Small ones are juicier and seedless, while the large, plump, glossy ones have more flavour and are easier to cook. Always handle them very carefully so that you do not bruise them.

Buckets of water placed beneath aubergines help create a humid atmosphere. This benefits the plants and discourages pests such as red spider mite.

Recommended varieties

'Black Enorma F$_1$', 'Rima F$_1$', 'Short Tom', 'Slice Rite No. 23 F$_1$'.

Advice from our expert – *on keeping aubergines healthy*

It is a far cry from Anastasis Stylianou's allotment in Muswell Hill to his childhood home in Cyprus, where he learned to grow aubergines at his father's knee. He feels the secret in England is 'keeping an eye on them the whole time'.

● Check the plants daily.
● Water at the first sign of wilting
● Spray the leaves with a solution of washing-up liquid as soon as you spot any aphids.
● Discourage pests by giving maximum ventilation on warm days.
● Maintain the humidity by placing buckets of water beneath the plants.
● If a plant looks sickly and the tops start to die, cut off the top. It may revive and produce new shoots from the stems.

Use

Preparation for cooking

Aubergines are best pre-salted before cooking. Cut them into slices or cubes, depending on the recipe, sprinkle with salt and leave for 30–60 minutes. Wipe them clean or rinse and pat dry.

Basic cooking methods

Aubergines can be deep-fried, sautéed, stir-fried, steamed or grilled. They can be incorporated into vegetable casseroles (they combine beautifully with tomatoes) and meat dishes such as moussaka. They are also good puréed, preserved in strips in olive oil or made into sweet pickles. Most aubergine dishes are excellent either hot or cold.

Sautéed aubergine (Melanzane al funghetto)

This very simple but excellent recipe comes from southern Italy, where its name means 'aubergines cooked like mushrooms'.

Serves 3–4

1 large aubergine
salt
olive oil for frying
2 cloves garlic, peeled and chopped
3 tbsp chopped fresh parsley
freshly ground black pepper

Cut the aubergine into 2 cm ($^3/_4$ in) cubes. Place in a colander and sprinkle with salt. Leave for 1 hour, then rinse and pat dry. Heat a generous layer of olive oil over a low to moderate heat in a large frying pan. Fry the aubergine gently, turning, until almost tender. Add the garlic and half the parsley, and fry for a few minutes longer until the aubergine is browned and tender. Season with pepper and a little more salt if necessary, and serve sprinkled with the remaining parsley.

---

gardening terms and techniques

Italicised words indicate a separate entry

Annual
A plant that grows from seed, completing its life cycle in one year and dying after seeding.

Aphids
Common insect pests including greenfly, blackfly and whitefly. Spray early with soft soap or diluted detergent; use biological control against whitefly in greenhouses.

Base dressing
A general fertiliser forked into the soil before sowing or planting.

Bed system
Growing vegetables in permanent individual beds, perhaps 1.2 m (4 ft) wide, with plants at equidistant spacing instead of in rows. Fertile soil is built up by working in manure, and by never treading on the soil (which destroys its structure). (See also *Raised beds.*)

Biological control
Using a natural enemy to control a pest or disease. Whitefly and *red spider mite* are commonly controlled by these means. (See Chase Organics under 'Suppliers', p. 54.)

Birds
Small birds eat seedlings; large birds often destroy brassicas. Protect against small birds by running a single strand of strong black cotton just above the seedlings. Netting crops is the only way of protecting them against large birds.

Blackfly See *Aphids.*

Blanching
Growing a plant in the dark or covering it to exclude light in order to make it white and more tender.

Bolting
Producing flowers and seed prematurely, often caused by cold or dry conditions or certain daylengths.

Brassicas
Vegetables in the cabbage family, e.g. cauliflower, Brussels sprouts, broccoli, kohlrabi, turnips, swedes, radish, oriental greens, kales.

Broadcast
A basic method of sowing outdoors. Make sure the *seedbed* is weed-free. Rake the soil to a fine *tilth* then scatter seed evenly over the surface. Rake in one direction then at right angles to cover it.

Cabbage root fly
The small white maggots of this fly eat the roots of brassicas. To prevent attacks put rubberised root fly discs around the stems of brassicas when planting or grow under fine *nets* to keep out the flies.

Carrot root fly
The most common carrot pest. The small, yellowish maggots of the fly eat the roots of carrots, parsley and celery. Destroy infested plants in the autumn to prevent overwintering, and prevent attack by growing the plants under fine *nets* or *fleecy films* and surrounding them with a barrier about 60 cm (2 ft) high.

Caterpillars
The caterpillars of cabbage white butterflies and various moths cause extensive damage, mainly on *brassicas*. Watch out for eggs and newly hatched caterpillars and destroy them by hand or spray with derris or pyrethrum. Alternatively, grow plants under protective *nets*.

Clamp See *Storage.*

Cloches
Portable structures of glass or plastic film in wire, metal or wood frames used to cover and protect crops.

Clubroot
A serious soil-borne disease which affects *brassicas*; the roots become grossly swollen and plants eventually die. It is difficult to eradicate, but liming acid soils and improving drainage help to prevent it. Where soil is infected raise plants in pots and transplant rather than sowing *in situ*. This head start may mean they can be harvested before they are infected.

Compost
Plant material that is collected together and rotted down, then dug back into the soil or applied as a *mulch*. It is an invaluable source of *organic matter* and *nutrients*. Make it piled up in a heap, covered finally with a tarpaulin, or in a bin (minimum: 1 m /3 ft square) constructed on three sides of breeze blocks, timber, straw bales or brick. The larger the

bin, the better it is insulated, and the more the ingredients are mixed together, the faster the compost will be made. The term 'compost' is also used for *sowing compost* and *potting compost.*

Container
Any pot, box or bucket used to grow plants. Large vegetables need pots at least 25 cm (10 in) in diameter. Containers must be filled with good soil or potting compost. Leave headroom for mulching and topdressing. Good drainage is essential; drill drainage holes low down on the side of flat-bottomed containers to prevent stagnation.

Cut-and-come-again
Productive method of growing mainly salad crops, to get several cuts of tasty, nutritious seedlings. Best sown in wide *drills.*

Damping down
Sprinkling greenhouses with water to lower the temperature and increase humidity in hot weather. Use a watering can or a hose with a sprinkler attachment, or you can simply partially block it with your thumb to create a spray.

Damping off
Attacks by parasitic fungi which cause small seedlings to keel over and die. Avoid by sowing thinly in warm soil in clean seedtrays and providing good ventilation.

Dibber
Rounded tool for making planting holes. Small dibbers are used for *pricking out.*

Disease
Few plant diseases are curable, but most can be avoided by good gardening practices. Strong plants outgrow or avoid disease. Build up *soil fertility,* never sow in cold, wet conditions, only plant strong, healthy plants, keep greenhouses well-ventilated, maintain high levels of garden hygiene and clear away weeds and debris. Some plants have 'disease resistance' – i.e. they have been bred with a useful degree of immunity to common diseases. (See also *Virus diseases.*)

Double digging
A method of digging the soil to two 'spits' or spade depths. It is recommended in new gardens, and from time to time on heavy soils. Working along the bed, take out a trench one spit deep (keep the soil for the final strip), fork over the bottom, then fill in the trench with soil from the adjacent strip.

Work in *organic matter* at all levels as you dig.

Drainage
Good drainage is essential for vegetable growing. In new gardens poor drainage may be caused by a compacted layer in the soil; this must be broken up with a pick-axe. Most drainage problems can be remedied by digging 60 cm (2 ft) deep trench drains across poorly drained areas. Fill the bottom 30 cm (1 ft) with stone and rubble before replacing the soil. Constantly digging in *organic matter* improves drainage remarkably.

Drill
A narrow furrow made in the soil in which seed is sown. The depth depends on the type of seed. In wet conditions line the drill with *sowing compost* or *potting compost* before sowing. In dry weather water the base of the drill only before sowing, put in the seed, then cover it with dry soil. This prevents evaporation and keeps the seed moist until germination.

Earthing up
Drawing soil around the stems of plants with a spade or hoe to support them, blanch them, or, in the case of potatoes, to prevent tubers being exposed to light and greening as a result.

Eelworm See *Nematodes*

F₁ hybrids
Plant varieties bred by crossing selected, inbred parent lines. The resulting plants have exceptional vigour and yields. Seed is expensive as the process has to be repeated whenever seed is required.

Fertilisers
These are used to supply the main *nutrients* that plants need or to boost growth. Easiest to apply are all-purpose concentrated chemical compounds such as Growmore or Phostrogen which are diluted and watered on the soil. *Organic* gardeners use natural fertilisers like *seaweed extracts* (for example Maxicrop) or fish, blood and bonemeal, which act more slowly.

Flea beetle
A common pest that damages *brassicas,* radishes and salad rocket at the seedling stage by nibbling holes in the leaves. It is easily controlled with derris dust or spray.

Fleecy films
Very light, soft, well-aerated films (for example

Agryl P 17, Envirofleece) which are laid directly over crops. They are mainly used early in the season to raise the temperature and protect from winds so that plants grow faster; they also give protection against some insects. Anchor the edges in slits in the soil or weight them down. They should normally be removed after six to eight weeks. Seedlings and crops can be covered with fleece to protect them from light frost. (See Suppliers, p. 55.)

Floating mulches
Fleecy films or *perforated plastic films* laid directly over plants.

Foliar feeds
Liquid fertilisers that are watered on to the plant's leaves. They are mainly used to correct trace element deficiencies (see *Nutrients*). *Seaweed extracts* are also often applied as foliar feeds.

Frames
Wood, brick, concrete or metal structures covered with glass or plastic film. They are used to protect crops and harden off seedlings.

Gentle heat See *Propagators*.

Grafting
A method of joining the shoot of one plant to the rootstock of another. Tomato varieties can be grafted on to rootstocks that are resistant to soil-borne diseases. Angled slits are made in both stems, which are bound with fine tape so the tissues grow together.

Greenfly See *Aphids*.

Hardening off
Gradually acclimatising plants raised indoors to colder temperatures to prevent 'shock' when planted out. It is done over two weeks by gradually increasing ventilation and/or moving them outside or into *frames* for increasingly long periods during the day.

Hardy
A description of plants that can survive frost in the open.

In situ
Sowing directly in the ground where the plant will grow, as opposed to sowing elsewhere and *transplanting*.

Intercropping
The practice of growing a fast and a slow crop side by side, or within the same row, to save space. The faster-growing crop is cleared first, allowing the other to mature. Low-growing, shade-tolerant vegetables can be grown to maturity under tall vegetables like sweet corn.

Liming See *Soil acidity*.

Liquid feeds
Fertilisers that are diluted and watered on to the soil around plants.

Manures
Manures are bulky natural products that break down in the soil into *organic matter*, with enormously beneficial effects on *soil fertility*. Animal manures, well-rotted straw, compost, spent mushroom compost and seaweed are excellent manures. Dig them into the soil in autumn, or mulch the soil in the growing season. It is almost impossible to work in too much manure.

Micro-propagation
The technique of raising plants from tissue in laboratory conditions to get disease-free, exceptionally high-quality plants.

Modules
Small units in which seeds are sown and grown until the potting or planting stage, so avoiding root disturbance. Top-quality plants result. Examples are small pots, 'Jiffy 7s' (small pots of compressed peat), seedtrays divided into compartments, moulded plastic or polystyrene trays with round or square holes or cells, and soil blocks made with hand blocking tools. Fill with module compost or *potting compost*, sow 2–3 seeds per cell and thin to the strongest after germination. (See Suppliers, p. 55.)

Mulch
A layer of material laid on the soil around plants. Use clear plastic film mulches to warm up the soil; black plastic mulches to keep down weeds and retain moisture in the soil; combined black and white plastic mulches to reflect light up to ripening fruit and suppress weed growth below. To plant through mulching films, lay the films on the ground, anchor them in the soil, cut crosses in the film and plant through them. Use organic mulches (e.g. compost, straw, rotted lawn mowings, etc.) in layers at least 5 cm (2 in) deep to conserve moisture, increase soil fertility and suppress weeds.

Nematodes (eelworms)
Highly damaging, microscopic soil pests for which there is no remedy other than rotation and growing resistant varieties where available.

Nets
Fine nets erected over low hoops give shelter and protection from many insect pests such as aphids, caterpillars and *cabbage and carrot root flies*. (See *Polytunnels* and Suppliers, p. 55.)

Nutrients
The key 'foods' for plant growth are nitrogen (N), phosphorus (P) and potassium (K): magnesium, calcium and sulphur are required in lesser amounts and *trace elements* are needed in tiny quantities only. Fertile soils have good reserves of elements, but nitrogen is washed out easily and supplies need to be replenished with *fertilisers* or *organic matter* which is converted into nitrogen in the soil.

Organic gardening
Gardening without the use of artificial fertilisers, weedkillers or chemical sprays other than those that break down rapidly into harmless products. Building up *soil fertility* is the key to successful organic gardening.

Organic matter
Any material of plant or animal origin that will break down in the soil, releasing *nutrients* and improving *soil structure*. It can be dug into the soil or spread on the surface as a mulch.

Pelleted seed
Seeds coated to make tiny balls which are easy to handle and sow spaced out, thus avoiding the need for thinning. They must be kept reasonably moist or they won't germinate.

Perennials
Plants that live for an indefinite period.

Perforated plastic films
Plastic films with holes or slits in them. They are used like *fleecy films* to encourage early growth, but must be removed after a few weeks or growth is restricted. They are cheaper than fleecy films.

pH See *Soil acidity*.

Planting
A few guidelines: Plant in cool conditions. Water the plant and the soil beforehand. Handle plants by the leaves, not the roots. Make a hole with a trowel, and put in the plant so that the lowest leaves are just above the soil level. Fill in the hole carefully, using fingertips to firm the soil around the plant. Give a leaf a gentle tug to make sure the plant is firm. In very hot weather, shade plants until established. To plant through mulching films, lay films on the ground, anchor them in the soil, cut crosses in the film, and plant through them.

Plastic films See *Mulches*.

Pollen beetle
Increasingly common tiny beetle which attacks the flowerheads of *brassicas* and other vegetables. If it is a serious problem in your area grow vegetables under *nets* or spray with derris.

Pollination
The transfer of pollen on to the stigma of a flower so the fruit will set. Usually done by insects or wind. High temperatures and dry atmosphere in greenhouses may kill pollen so fruits fail to set.

Polytunnels
The poor man's greenhouse. 'Walk-in' tunnels roughly 1.8 m (6 ft) high, made from heavy polythene film laid over steel pipe hoops and buried in the soil at the edges. With care film lasts three years. Polytunnels are easily dismantled and erected on a new site to prevent *soil sickness* developing. 'Low tunnels' – on average 50 cm (20 in) high – are made from light polythene film over wire or steel hoops. They are the cheapest form of *protection* early and late in the season. Tie the film around stakes at either end. (See illustration on p. 25 and Suppliers, p. 55)

Potting compost
The mixture into which plants are grown when *pricked out, potted up* or *potted on*. Soil-based mixtures like John Innes include soil, peat, sand and *nutrients*. Many composts are based on peat or peat substitutes.

Potting on
Transferring a plant from one pot into a larger one.

Potting up
Transferring a seedling from the seedtray or pot in which it was sown into an individual pot.

Pre-germinated seed
Seed which is germinated (or chitted) before it is sown to overcome poor soil conditions. Place the seed on a damp paper towel in a warm place and sow carefully when the tiny root appears. Varieties

that are tricky to germinate are sometimes sold pre-germinated.

Pricking out
Gently uprooting young seedlings and spacing them further apart in a seedtray or in a single pot. Hold them by the leaves rather than the roots as the delicate root hairs are easily damaged. The pricking-out stage can be avoided by sowing in *modules* or sowing seeds spaced far apart in seedtrays.

Primed seed
Seed which is brought to the point of germination, then dried, before being packeted. Once sown it germinates very rapidly.

Propagate
To raise a plant, either from seed or by a vegetative method.

Propagators
Electrically heated devices used to supply bottom heat for germination. In the simplest type, a light bulb is set beneath a seedtray with a domed cover to create a moist atmosphere. 'Gentle heat' is a temperature of 13–16 °C (55–60 °F).

Protection
A general term for covers which improve growing conditions and plant quality, e.g. *floating mulches, polytunnels, cloches, frames* and greenhouses.

Raised beds
Beds that are 30 cm (12 in) or so above ground level. They give improved *drainage* and better exposure to sun. (See also *Bed system*.)

Red spider mite
Tiny, potentially very serious pest, especially in greenhouses. Ventilation and spraying to lower temperatures help prevent its build-up. It is resistant to many chemical sprays, so *biological control* is used to control it.

Ridging up soil
A method of exposing heavy soil to winter frosts which break it down. To make ridges on a narrow bed, fork down the centre, then fork the soil on each side over the centre. Adapt this process to larger beds. Ridged beds can be covered with straw or manure during the winter. The worms will work it into the soil. (See also *Soil structure*.)

Root offsets
Sections of a root system, obtained by pulling a root apart, so that each section will grow into a separate plant.

Rotation
Where crops from the same botanical family are grown on the same ground for several consecutive years, certain serious pests and diseases may develop. To avoid this, the crops are rotated around the garden over at least a four-year cycle, if possible. For example, the vegetable garden can be divided into four areas, in each of which one main group is grown in turn. Fit miscellaneous vegetables such as salads into any convenient spaces that arise. The main botanical groups are: *brassicas*, potato family (includes tomatoes and peppers), onion family (includes leeks and garlic), pea and bean family. If rotation is impossible because a garden is too small, avoid growing crops on the same soil two years running.

Seaweed extracts
The various fertilisers based on seaweed are low in *nutrients*, but nevertheless seem to have very beneficial effects on plants, possibly through supplying *trace elements* and other growth-promoting substances.

Seed leaves
The first leaf or pair of leaves (cotyledons) to appear when a seedling germinates. They are often quite different in appearance from the true leaves that follow.

Seed viability
Seed viability (ability to germinate) declines over time, depending on the type and how it is stored. Always keep seed in dry, cool conditions (a fridge is ideal); as a general rule don't use seed that is over three years old.

Seedbed
A piece of ground prepared for sowing by being raked down until it is a fine *tilth*. The term is also used for an area set aside for sowing seeds which are later transplanted into their permanent positions. Seedbeds should be weed-free if possible or seedlings may be swamped by weeds. To make them weed-free prepare the ground several weeks in advance, cover with clear plastic to encourage weeds to germinate, and hoe off the weeds before sowing.

Sideshoots
Shoots which come off the main stems. On tall tomatoes (but not bush types) they must be

nipped out to concentrate energy into the *trusses* on the main stem.

Slugs

Very serious pests, feeding mainly on the leaves of a wide range of crops; young plants and the softer-leaved *brassicas* are especially vulnerable. Control with chemical or organic slug pellets, scattered on the soil among plants. Slugs are night-feeders and are easily collected by torchlight.

Soil acidity

This is measured on the pH scale, with pH7 being neutral. The lower the number, the more acid the soil. Slightly acid soil (pH 6–6.5) suits most vegetables. British soils are tending to become increasingly acid. If growth is poor and tests reveal low pH, raise it over two or three years by liming. Dig in ground limestone in autumn at an average rate of 450 g/sq m (1 lb/sq yd). Only lime if really necessary; working in plenty of organic matter normally prevents the problem arising. Use soil-testing kits and meters to test your soil. (See Suppliers, p. 55.)

Soil blocks

A useful type of *module*, made by compressing soil- or peat-based compost into cubes with a hand blocker. (See Suppliers, p. 55.)

Soil fertility

A fertile soil is rich in *organic matter* and *nutrients*, well-drained and well-aerated. There is no short cut to building up fertility: it is just a matter of working in as much organic matter as possible. Whatever the soil type, this encourages earthworms and leads to an improvement in *soil structure*.

Soil sickness

Diseases develop in soils where the same crop is grown year after year. Soil sickness is most common in greenhouses, with the tomato, pepper, and aubergine family.

Soil structure

Refers to the way in which soil particles are held together in different-sized crumbs. The ideal loamy soil is a mixture of soil types and humus. Extreme soil types are heavy clays (tiny particles) and sandy soils (large particles). Both gradually become good loams with the addition of *organic matter*. Soils with good structure are 'workable', i.e. easily prepared in spring by lightly forking the ground and raking it to a good *tilth*. Heavy clay soils should be dug and ridged in winter to improve structure; light sandy soils are better mulched and dug over in spring.

Soil temperature

Soil temperature can be measured with a soil thermometer. Most seeds need at least 7 °C (45 °F) to germinate; some need higher temperatures. Warm up soils in spring by covering with cloches or clear plastic film. It is always better to delay sowing than to sow in cold soil.

Sowing compost

A fine-textured compost with few nutrients, used to sow seedlings. Where unavailable sow in general purpose compost or *potting compost*.

Sowing indoors

Term for sowing under cover to give plants an early start, often in a *propagator*. The basic method is to sow in a seedtray or small container, *pricking out* into small pots or larger containers then *potting on* later if necessary. (See also *modules*.) You need sufficient space to keep the seedlings in good light and moderately warm before they are planted out. (See also *Sowing compost* and *Potting compost*.)

Sowing in succession

Making frequent sowings to ensure a continuous supply. As a rough guide, make the next sowing when the previous sowing is through the soil.

Sowing outdoors

Sowing direct in the ground, *in situ* or in a *seedbed* for transplanting. Most seeds are sown in *drills* or *broadcast*.

Sowing under cover

Sowing in protected conditions, such as in a greenhouse, *polytunnel*, *frame* or under *cloches*. (See also *Sowing indoors*.)

Station sowing

Sowing seeds in clusters of two to four seeds along a drill, rather than continuously, to make thinning easier. Sow clusters at half the final spacing, e.g. in groups 10 cm (4 in) apart if the final spacing will be 20 cm (8 in) apart.

Stopping

Nipping out the growing point of a plant. Tomatoes are stopped a couple of leaves above the top *truss* to prevent further growth so that the remaining tomatoes will mature.

Storage

Store root vegetables like carrots in layers, in

slightly moist sand or sieved ashes in boxes or bins. Keep in a frost-free shed or store them outside in clamps. Start with a 15 cm (6 in) layer of straw, pile the vegetables on top, and cover with a similar layer of straw topped with 15cm (6 in) of soil.

Tender
A plant which cannot stand any frost.

Thinning
Removing surplus seedlings after sowing *in situ*. Thin when the soil is damp; never let seedlings get overcrowded; thin in stages so each seedling is clear of its neighbour; pinch off at ground level to minimise root disturbance.

Tilth
A fine crumbly surface suitable for sowing, obtained by raking the soil.

Top dressing
Applying *fertilisers*, *compost* or soil around a plant during its growing season, primarily to supply extra *nutrients*.

Trace elements
Plant *nutrients* required in minute quantities, normally present in fertile soil. Where deficiencies cause problems spray with appropriate trace element *foliar feed*.

Transplanting
Transferring a plant from one piece of ground to another, from a pot into the ground or from a smaller to a larger pot.

Truss
A cluster of flowers or fruits.

Virus diseases
A range of incurable diseases which are transmitted from plant to plant, often by insects or by introducing diseased material. Always buy healthy, certified plants where available. Burn any plants affected by a virus disease.

Watering
Water seedlings and very young plants gently and frequently. With established plants an occasional thorough watering is far better than frequent light watering. Mulching the soil cuts down on the need for watering.

Weeds
Must be kept at bay as they compete with vegetables for light, nutrients and moisture. Control annual weeds by hoeing or pulling up by hand. It is essential to prevent them from seeding. Control perennial weeds by digging them up. Black plastic mulches are excellent for preventing weed germination. Weedkillers are generally not recommended or necessary in vegetable gardens.

Windbreaks
Protecting plants from even light winds increases yields by 20 per cent. Funnelling winds, for example those between buildings, are especially damaging to plants. Windbreaks provide shelter over a distance roughly six times their height. They should be 50 per cent solid so winds are filtered rather than completely stopped. Hedges, lath or wattle fences and nylon windbreak netting battened to strong posts are commonly used windbreaks.

Whitefly See *Aphids*.

resources

further reading

Vegetables

The Kitchen Garden: a historical guide to traditional crops by David Stuart, Alan Sutton Publishing, 1987.

The Salad Garden by Joy Larkcom, Frances Lincoln Ltd/Windward, 1984.

The Vegetable Garden Displayed by Joy Larkcom, Royal Horticultural Society, 1992.

Oriental Vegetables by Joy Larkcom, John Murray, 1991.

General interest

Royal Horticultural Society Encyclopedia of Gardening, ed. Christopher Brickell, Dorling Kindersley Ltd, 1992.

The Complete Small Garden by Graham Rice, Papermac, 1991.

The Vegetable Finder, ed. Jeremy Cherfas, HDRA, 1993. Highly recommended. Lists up-to-date sources of vegetable seed and some plants.

Organic gardening

The Complete Manual of Organic Gardening, ed. Basil Caplan, Headline Book Publishing, 1992.

The Organic Garden by Sue Stickland, Hamlyn, 1992.

Bob Flowerdew's Complete Book of Companion Gardening by Bob Flowerdew, Kyle Cathie, 1993.

The Organic Gardener by Bob Flowerdew, Hamlyn, 1993.

The Permaculture Way by Graham Bell, Thorsons, 1992.

HDRA Step by Step series of leaflets on organic gardening methods. 50p each from Chase Organics (see below). Subjects include: organic gardening, composting, worm compost, pest control, mulching, growing from seed, weed control, slugs, green manures, starting an allotment, comfrey, herbs in containers, oriental brassicas, the organic greenhouse.

---

suppliers

Seeds

All these companies will send free seed catalogues on request. Specialities, and varieties mentioned in the programmes that are available from only one or two sources, are given in brackets.

Bakker Seeds, PO Box 111, Spalding, Lincs. PE12 6EL
(General list)

J. W. Boyce, Bush Pasture, Lower Carter St, Fordham, Ely, Cambs. CB7 5JU
(General list)

D. T. Brown, Poulton-le-Fylde, Blackpool, Lancs. FY6 7HY
(General, 'Abunda' tomato, Texsel greens)

John Chambers, 15 Westleigh Rd, Barton Seagrave, Kettering, Northants NN15 5AJ
(Edible wild plants, salads)

Chase Organics, Coombelands House, Coombelands Lane, Addlestone, Weybridge Surrey KT15 1HY
(General, 'Oriental Saladini', organic books & sundries, biological control agents)

Chiltern Seeds, Bortree Stile, Ulverston, Cumbria LA12 7PB
(Specialities: unusual and oriental vegetables)

Dig & Delve Organics, Fen Road, Blo' Norton, Diss, Norfolk IP22 2JH
(General, oriental, organic books & sundries)

Dobies Seeds, Broomhill Way, Torquay, Devon TQ2 7QW
(General, oriental, sundries)

Mr Fothergill Seeds, Gazeley Rd, Kentford, Newmarket, Suffolk CB8 7QB
(General list)

HDRA, National Centre for Organic Gardening, Ryton on Dunsmore, Coventry CV8 3LG
(Old varieties, e.g. 'Red and White' French bean, available to members from seed library)

W. W. Johnson, London Rd, Boston, Lincs. PE21 8AD
(General and 'Mantanghong' radish)

Kings of Kelvedon, Monks Farm, Coggeshall Rd,
Kelvedon, Essex CO5 9PG
(General, oriental, organic sundries)

S. E. Marshall, Wisbech, Cambs. PE13 2RF
(General, sundries, 'Feurio' ruby chard in 1994)

Poynzfield Herb Nursery, Black Isle, by Dingwall,
Ross-shire IV7 8LX
(Unusual vegetable and herb seed and plants; send
SAE and 3 first-class stamps)

Proseed, 26 Chapman Close, Potton, Sandy,
Beds. SG19 2PL
(Specialist: commercial varieties)

W. Robinson & Sons, Sunnybank, Forton,
Nr Preston, Lancs. PR3 0BN
(Giant vegetables, 'Mammoth' onion, 'Britain's
Breakfast' tomato)

Suffolk Herbs, Monks Farm, Coggeshall Rd
Kelvedon, Essex CO5 9PG
(General, herbs, Continental salads, 'Oriental
Saladini', 'Bisai' and 'Munchen Bier' radish,
sundries)

Suttons Seeds, Hele Rd, Torquay,
Devon TQ2 7QJ
(General, sundries)

Thompson & Morgan, London Rd,
Ipswich, Suffolk IP2 0BA
(General, 'Sungold' tomato)

Unwins Seeds, Histon, Cambridge CB4 4LE
(General, sundries, 'Sioux' tomato)

Plants
Asparagus
Ken Muir, Honeypot Farm, Rectory Rd,
Weeley Heath, Clacton-on-Sea,
Essex CO16 9BJ
(Micro-propagated varieties)

Michael Paske Farms, The Estate Office,
Honington, Grantham, Lincs. NG32 2PG
(Wide range including hybrids)

Comfrey
Chase Organics (see *Seeds*)

Potatoes
S. E. Marshall (see *Seeds*)

Websters Seed Potatoes, 8 Denside, Letham
Grange, Arbroath, Tayside DD11 4QI

Equipment
Agralan, The Old Brickyard, Ashton Keynes
Swindon, Wilts. SN6 6QR
(Fleecy films, nets, low tunnels)

Ladbrooke Engineering, The Bank,
Bidford-on-Avon, Alcester, Warwicks. B50 4NL
(Soil blockers)

LBS Polythene, Cottontree, nr Colne,
Lancs. BB8 7BW
(Polytunnels, plastics, mulches, fleecy films)

PG Horticulture, Street Farm, Thornham Magna,
Eye, Suffolk IP23 8HB
(Modular trays, low tunnel system, nets)

Rapitest, London Road, Corwen, Clywd LL21 0DR
(Soil-testing kits)

Organisations
National Centre for Organic Gardening
Ryton on Dunsmore, Coventry CV8 3LG

Royal Horticultural Society
80 Vincent Square, London SW1P 2PE

Published in 1993 by
Channel 4 Television
60 Charlotte Street
London W1P 2AX

Produced by Broadcasting Support
Services to accompany *Grow Your Greens,
Eat Your Greens* (Wall to Wall Television
productions for Channel 4, produced by
Joanne Reay, directed by Basil Comely and
Alex Morengo and presented by Sophie
Grigson), first shown on Channel 4 in
April–May 1993.

Writer: Joy Larkcom
Editor: Derek Jones
Editorial consultant: Nancy Duin
Line drawings: Elizabeth Douglass
Cover photographs: David Palmer
Designer: Iris Wilkes, Shape of Things
Printer: Haynes Cannon

Distributed by Broadcasting Support
Services

Broadcasting Support Services is an
educational charity, which runs helplines
and provides follow-up services for
viewers and listeners.

For further copies, please send a cheque
or postal order for £3.50 (made payable to
Channel 4 Television) to:

Grow Your Greens
PO Box 4000
London W3 6XJ or Cardiff CF5 2XT